AN EDUCATION
Selected Writings by Luca and Friends

NICOLETTA STAME, EDITOR
A Colorni-Hirschman International Institute

BORDIGHERA PRESS
NEW YORK

Il nostro mezzogiorno

Volume 2

Translated from Italian by Michael Gilmartin

This book series is dedicated to the presentation of new perspectives on how we might re-consider Southern Italy.

Cover art: Pythagoras and Archimedes, detail from Raphael's *The School of Athens* in the Apostolic Palace, Vatican City, 1509–1511

ISBN 978-1-59954-226-3
Library of Congress Control Number: 2024944906

BORDIGHERA PRESS
NEW YORK

TABLE OF CONTENTS

Nicoletta Stame

INTRODUCTION

1. AN EXPERIENCE, A GROUP, AN INSPIRATION

This book is a collection of writings[1] related to an educational journey, one that includes both classroom work (as practiced by Luca Meldolesi, professor of economic policy at Federico II University in Naples, and his students), and the formation of a group[2] that has taken various names[3] in successive phases. In both cases the aim is to capture the original core and legacy of an experience that dates from the early 1990s and which—with its dropouts and new entries, with highs and lows that have seen it engaged in both government and business activities—is still going strong today.

What distinguishes this experience is its connection with the ideas of Albert Hirschman and Eugenio Colorni, and the ambition to reframe it as an active process of change, unfolding in a particular situation and a particular time. Its distinctiveness impels us to present it to the wider world, because we discern in it ideas that might encourage others to venture onto terrain that, while less traveled, holds promise for those who aspire to an experience of democracy and civilization—in the active sense of the word.

In practical terms, this means applying Hirschmanian ideas on development as a way of both unlocking personal energies and harnessing the positive and dynamic aspects of an environ-

---

[1] The texts collected here come for the most part from the brochures of *Italia Vulcanica*, edited between 2018 and 2022. The latter reprinted writings that had appeared in the *Bollettini* issued in the years of Luca Meldolesi's teaching in the 1990s.

[2] Almost as in a bildungsroman, not least reflected in the trials the group has had to face to grow stronger and more mature.

[3] Association, Experimental promotion group, Room 22, Committee, Committee for the Emergence of Nonregular Labor, Democratic Federalism, and today A Colorni-Hirschman International Institute.

ment like the Mezzogiorno, which labors under a burden of negative esteem. This can be achieved by setting up a collective task which, while stimulating students to look closely at their own local environment, produces knowledge[4] that empowers them to aim higher, to fit into the larger community as a constant frame of reference (from Cardoso's Brazil to the intellectual world inspired by Hirschman).[5]

The line of reasoning moves between dimensions that are political and psychological. The political dimension is situated in an avowedly development-oriented collective project (working groups, joint research). It also involves promoting a different way of looking at the surrounding environment (from neighborhood businesses to the Mezzogiorno in general), and teaching "practical and democratic political economy." But this goes hand in hand with an interpretation of the psychological side of development. This may be found both in Luca's reflections on his own personal experience and in the students' psychological work on illusion and disappointment, and desire and reality—continually shifting between the Mezzogiorno's condition and their own. In Vincenzo's words, it is the "focus on the psychological aspects of change [...] that subverts the tendency toward disillusionment, toward 'fracasomania.'"[6]

We need to move in two directions. On one hand, the focus needs to be on the difficulties, the negative aspects (the scourges, the barbarity), in order to be able to fight them. This includes identifying their weak points instead of excusing them

---

[4] The next two volumes in this series, *A Practical and Democratic Social Science* and *Our Mezzogiorno*, are dedicated to the key findings of this research.

[5] From Judith Tendler, who welcomed to MIT's DUSP those students who intended to pursue graduate studies, to Catherine and Pierre Grémion of Sciences Po (Paris), to Osvaldo Feinstein (World Bank). All of them also participated in a series of seminars at the Institute of Philosophical Studies in Naples, organized by the Chair in "Economic Policy".

[6] "Sovversione e auto-sovversione," [subversion and self-subversion], in Part II below.

and adapting to them (this is the theme of welfarism and "everybody does it"). And secondly, we need to know how to tap into the positive aspects—the desire to learn, the readiness to work hard, and the need to unlock these situations and make full use of their potential.

The volume contains mostly writings of Luca's reflecting on how the work in progress is evolving, but we also get a sense (through the writings of others as well) of the troubled experience of the group of people who were initially students in the "Economic Policy" course, then wrote "super-theses," became supervisors of other thesis students, and—even when they took on outside employment—remained part of the association, dedicated to strengthening their own practical activity, their research, and their links with others. It is a group that, by identifying with the thinking of Hirschman and Colorni, adopts a possibilist lexicon that includes "slack," "inverted sequences," "cognitive dissonances," "meta-preferences," and "exit and voice," but then does not hesitate to invent its own, as much in the analysis of "scourges" as in the strategies of the "affective method," the "magical divide," or "towing with headway" (a nautical metaphor, copyright Paolo Di Nola).

The organization of the volume reflects these different facets and dimensions.

2.   A CONSTELLATION OF CIRCUMSTANCES

The first part has a mostly historical bent. It is a backward look at how it was possible for the story to take hold—what constellation of circumstances (to use a term dear to Hirschman) fostered it. Luca Meldolesi, with a wealth of experience behind him as a theoretical economist steeped in the lessons of a "sui generis" economist like Hirschman and close to Hirschman's friends in Latin America committed to their countries' return to democracy, teaches in an economics department that—in part because of its location—attracts students from the Neapolitan hinterland. This is a dynamic periphery, an area which at the time in question (the end of state welfare in the 1980s, the fall of the Berlin Wall and the ensuing developments in the German economy) saw the growth of small and medium-sized businesses, including in the form of semi-district aggregates, that produced typical made-in-Italy goods (for the individual and the home). These business facts are ignored by official economics (even as taught in the same department) because, despite being capable of producing exports, they are "invisible," attracting instead the attention of "industrial district" economists, with whom the group has an intense dialogue. It is here that the attention and research in Luca's practical and democratic economic policy course is concentrated. And those who live in these settings, whether as students or as the subjects and the object of this research, contribute to their own empowerment even as they overcome their own atavistic sense of "inadequacy."

The inaugural lecture of Luca's economic policy course presents the program of the cultural break that is being proposed. Starting with the concept of the "discovery" of the "possible," the lecture ranges be-tween central themes of social science (knowledge of the object and the self, surprise, the limits of economic models, the morality of the social sciences) and references to a real-world setting such as Cardoso's Brazil, which allows students to see themselves as part of an international community of purpose, and to track the evidence of a skillful struggle against intransigence.

3. TEACHING AND ORGANIZATION

The second part takes us directly into the dynamics of the group, and how the theoretical side of the experience is shaped. The first three chapters are a striking example of Luca's original reworking of Colornian-Hirschmanian concepts, and the continuous trespassing between economics and psychology.

"My Idea about Slack" starts with the Hirschmanian concept of slack, the basis of *The Strategy of Economic Development* (Hirschman, 1958). Unearthing the existing reserve of "hidden, scattered and badly utilized" resources and mobilizing them for development is the strategy that Luca applies to himself and to his work with students—a way of getting them unstuck, which was also the spark for building the group.

"The Affective Method," evoking Colorni's theory of love,[7] is the other aspect of slack. It is based on the principle of "giving in order to receive." It is about the recipient, the one who is unblocked, who will then have to "learn to give, to give more than he or she receives."[8] Generosity in giving, in whatever field and activity, does not call for gratitude, but for behavior that promotes the development of others.

"A Magical Divide" invokes the interplay between exit and voice, a classic Hirschmanian theme, and applies it to the situation of moving between slack and unblocking. The "magical divide," is also the *"punctum gaudens"* between these two conditions, the oxygen-producing moment of recovery from depression.

The chapters that follow, beginning with "Making Affect Work," present a practical enactment of these formulations. Here we see the characters moving about the stage—with their activities, their interpersonal dynamics, and their interactions with the outside world.

A good part of these chapters concerns the relationship between Luca and the students—an asymmetric relationship that aims to achieve a positive exchange. Luca claims he does not want to be seen as "Rambo," but as a figure to compare oneself with as a means of strengthening one's autonomy

---

[7] See the chapter "The Strength and Vitality of Love" in Colorni (2019: 83-92).

[8] In "Subversion and self-subversion," Vincenzo Marino takes up this theme as regards towing with headway: "conversion from more or less heavy towing devices into powerful tractors capable of pulling other people."

("Giving Everything"). And Stefania Squillante ("Passions and Interests") recognizes that the commitment "to the common cause (possibilism, association, research)" that Luca asks of them is rewarded by their own self-esteem and empowerment.

In other chapters, the relationship with the students is set in the difficult environment of Naples, where coping requires high moral standards ("Environment and Psyche")—shunning prevailing trends, that is, and championing excellence. This requires performing "psychological maintenance" on oneself, in support of the individual change indispensable to the growth of one's own work and that of others. We gather that this issue kept the group busy for some time, since a later text ("Five Liberations") mentions the positive results of the "psychological campaign"—successfully overcoming one's own resistance, linking the teaching of economic policy to individual success, and learning how to manage the astuteness of exit-voice in dealings with the outside world.

Another group of chapters is dedicated to the collective activities of the group, the difficulties and rewards, their mechanisms and rules. These revolve around the idea of a "mentor" and of commitment in one's work, which Luca evokes in his relationship with Hirschman, and before that with Joan Robinson.

The "Satisfied Supervisor" describes one of the group's main activities, supervising "super-theses". Though demanding a great deal of effort from the student, the aim is to enhance student excellence. This chapter places supervision itself under the supervisor's lens, offering a broad overview of how supervisors themselves strengthen their own organizational and research skills, and how they build collaborative relationships with those under supervision, who in effect become part of the organization. "Subversion and self-subversion" links one's own transformation (self-subversion) with the mechanism of "towing with headway," which the Association uses with newcomers to unleash positive energies and suppress unsupportive attitudes. This theme is taken up in "About Who We Are and Where We Come From," recalling the Colornian idea of the "courage of innocence"[9] as a way of combating selfish and distrustful behavior with the example of democracy and respect.

Finally, "Spontaneity and Energy" raises the psychological question to the level of a theory of spontaneity, magnificently expressed in an article by Colorni.[10] It is a pivot to the succeeding section, picking up the issues of training and organization expressed in the students' own accounts, and leading into new post-graduation issues (graduates who have found jobs, public managers who are interested in our work). And it closes with a wish that sums up the psychological campaign: "What I would like to see added to all this is a keen perception of the issue of mobilizing individual energies as a specific and general problem to be tackled in an atmosphere of creativity, fond emulation and the most absolute freedom."

4. EDUCATION, RESEARCH AND CHANGE

The third section contains a series of key writings from this period that reflect economic and psychological themes debated within the group. They were inspired by observations from the students (as in the case of the Camorra) and by the need to maintain a high moral profile. The aim is to shed light on the negative elements in order to fight them better, to unearth "the traces, dialectics, and methodologies of possible change", in the belief that their increased visibility in the South helps bring them into focus as problems of the entire country.

"Recovering from the Camorra" is the section most closely tied to the daily experience of the students, who often find themselves side by side with the children of mobsters and have been

---

[9] As reads the title of a collection of Colorni's writings that Luca Meldolesi had edited at the time: Colorni (1998).

[10] "Spontaneity as a Form of Organization" in Colorni (2019: 25-32).

able to observe directly their movements and aspirations. In spite of the spread and diversification of the Camorra's activities and its negative impact on the local economy, the study sets before our eyes the dangerous life Camorrists lead and reveals that the culture of the Camorra is less robust than we think.

"Maladie d'amour" is a euphemism for "welfarism." Here we encounter another great source of inspiration, Ignazio Silone, who talks about the surprises (sic) of welfare. Here we see the mechanism by which the poor peasant's age-old humility and shame at asking for help has turned into a mind-numbing "scramble for subsidies." It is the desire to "live like a gentleman" (i.e., without working), which then "manifests itself in an underestimation of one's own abilities that creates the temptation to abuse power"[11] . In a world like the present one, with its claim to be more modern, the citizen is not motivated only by "self-interest," but also expects "benevolence" (to use the Smithian dichotomy), in an interweaving of market logic and "troglodytic" temptation. The individual constantly faces expressions of modernity that are "dissonant" with respect to the old mentality, which he or she can respond to by showing a capacity to change, but also by staking out a position of resistance, maintaining that modern society can be subjected to a rationale of violence.

"The three scourges" takes the entire issue to a level that is methodological and substantive at the same time. It is a lecture Luca gave to an audience of Tuscan "districtists," explaining the strategies invented to promote development in his own area. It begins with observations in the field and with the idea of surprise, defining the problem (the collective psychology of welfare dependency as a characteristic of the Italian crisis[12]), and goes on to thoroughly analyze the phenomenon of the three scourges (criminality, cronyism, corporatism), each of

---

[11] Silone (1968:90).
[12] Italian, not only southern

which has its own particular characteristics, nature and consequences, but whose boundaries are difficult to define. At the same time, these "barbaric" forms of behavior coexist alongside aspirations to normality and excellence (the desire for a clean South that means to rid itself of its ills), demonstrating that the reality is a composite of positive and negative factors, and that any analysis must aim to identify their intensity, continuity and direction. In dialogue with another privileged interlocutor, Manlio Rossi-Doria, and his metaphor of bone and flesh, it is noted that the hilly "bone" areas "have found in their peasant and artisan traditions the knowledge and values necessary for productive effort," while the flat "flesh" areas, recipients of massive public assistance, have been more interested in clientelist handouts, while also encouraging parasitic and criminal behavior. Thus bone and flesh are found mixed in the "beef stew" thesis—which recognizes the complexity, the "secrets and potentials, for better or worse," of different local systems.

5. EDUCATION AND BEYOND

The fourth part brings the circle of education to a close, so to speak, by addressing the themes of "post-graduation" and the "external environment," situations for which the educational experience was meant to be a preparation. But it projects it against the backdrop of the country as a whole, the "bumblebee"—in Becattini's words—that always appears to plummet, only to take flight once again. In the mixture of democracy and feudalism, merit and string-pulling that characterizes the country, success in fighting the negative pole is a condition for advancing the positive pole: "experiencing the future in the present, and sustaining the rise of modern, civilized Italy on a daily basis." This statement is aimed at young people who have studied and graduated, and who now find themselves in a work situation that may let them fall back into old habits. It is important to maintain links with them, as well as with students from previous generations and with anyone else who has related experiences, at whatever level, in "a team game involving a general orientation and specific qualitative and quantitative contributions." In their research and work activities they should strive to embody that mix of "model officials" and "model rebels" ("competent rebels" as Hirschman had it), which comes from being able, even in changing conditions, to make the most of the lessons learned in the course of their education, in accordance with the Hirschmanian theory of the "conservation and mutation of social energy." Luca has recently returned to this with a broad look that moves from the "high tide" of the 1990s—which are the object of this and the companion volumes in this series—to the goals of A Colorni-Hirschman International Institute today.

PART I

The Constellation of Circumstances. Or, how it was possible

Luca Meldolesi: *Preface to "Italia Vulcanica"* 1, 2018

Luca Meldolesi: *A constellation of favorable circumstances*, 2022

Luca Meldolesi: *Opening lesson of the course in economic policy, a.y. 1994-95*, 1995

Luca Meldolesi

Preface to *Italia Vulcanica* 1[1]

Experience tells us that great mass processes are highly relevant to human affairs—vigorously inseminating the social body, so that now and again, new saplings and further ventures may later spring forth. But in life's comings and goings it
is not easy to maintain a continuity of ideas and a constructive
presence. I sometimes wonder, for example, where the rebels
of the 1960s ended up. It appears to me that for the most part
they are dispersed and despondent—tamed by life. For Nicoletta Stame and me this has not been the case. We're still
here. How have we managed it? With patience, study, contem-
plation, and determination, certainly. With prudent professional and personal choices—of this there is no doubt. But also
with foreign connections, first and foremost with Albert
Hirschman. And thus, with generally favorable objective and
subjective conditions and with fertile constellations of circumstances—that are actually within our reach.

But to appreciate how this has been possible working in
the Naples area, in the South, in Rome, within centralized institutions, and around the world, it is perhaps useful to look at
our activities (intellectual, educational, intervention) *at the micro
level*, through the stratagems that we and our "circle" of friends,
students, and alumni have used over time. As we shall see,
some of our "tricks" are imports, others invented ad hoc; some
come from the Colornian-Hirschmanian tradition, others are a
mix, etc. They will perhaps help clarify (possibly indirectly)
how we have been able to survive for so long (and even pros-
per!) in a less than easy part of our country and in a professional

---

[1] From *Italia Vulcanica* n. 1 (2018): 5-6.

and political dimension that is not connected to the political system. We were not a movement (in the strict sense of the word); our university connection was used very freely; there were no extra economic benefits of any kind (far from it!), yet we were not part of the voluntary sector; we had no hierarchical structures; we did not use public money; and (partly by choice, partly by necessity) we were very frugal with private money as well. In other words, the experience shaped itself by degrees according to what we were able to do and what we wanted to do.

Our main invention was precisely this. Starting with university teaching in relatively backward conditions, we demonstrated on the ground that when the focus is on the intensive and enjoyable training of receptive students and on concrete intervention at the local level, it is possible (even if anything but easy) to build, in alternating stages, a long-term trajectory that ultimately leads both the participants and their experiences "upward," even professionally—to the point where it can gradually spill over regionally, nationally, and even abroad—potentially reaching many parts of the developed and developing world. Of course this is not the only way. Without doubt there are many other avenues for those who wish to build solid foundations of participatory federalist democracy. But the very fact that the one we chose (and stubbornly pursued for so many years) turned out in practice to be viable is undoubtedly "good news." And it already allows us to widen the spectrum of possibilities (and therefore the latitude of choice). On one hand it can point to similar paths, and on the other its very existence (unusual as it is) can encourage other pathways which, while perhaps very different, are implicitly linked to ours by the desire to act, concretely and from the heart, "for a better world."

Obviously, we did not move in a straight line or at a steady pace (on automatic pilot). On the contrary, we had to grapple with the daily grind, cautiously and with the patience of saints (and at different levels of awareness and involvement), navigating numerous tortuous individual and collective sets of circumstances—each of which (from prelude to conclusion) was marked by its own specific procedure (tied to concrete realities—including, of course, inevitable fluctuations in behavior). Each of these, in addition, driven as it was by the desire for private-public betterment, was marked by the continual effort to trigger the leap forward that we could feel within our reach. Under such conditions it was crucial to learn how to intelligently, even imperceptibly, "nudge the rudder" in each of the different initiatives to steer them in the desired direction. The purpose was to identify (and properly take advantage of) the small opportunities, the "gateways" to change, that successively presented themselves, and to contribute, combining resourcefulness with patience, to the success of such activities. This required reflection and constant updating concerning next steps, and stratagems either known or devised for the purpose—with the emphasis always on holding the participants' interest.

Luca Meldolesi
A Constellation of Favorable Circumstances[2]

The cultural climate [at the beginning of the 1990s] was favorable, thanks to the fall of the Berlin Wall (and to the development of a "district-oriented" literature in economics[3]). There was also a tortuous trend in the Italian economy. The end of the welfare high tide of the 1980s (which had driven the share of public spending in Southern income to an astronomical level) produced by the "squeeze" of 1992 (and "*Mani Pulite*" [Clean Hands]) had generated a dramatic economic and social repositioning in the Mezzogiorno. On one hand, it had put the traditional feeding trough of the Southern gentry on "short rations," and on the other, a severe curb on regular manufacturing activities had indirectly favored the semi-subterranean, household and personal goods businesses of southern SMEs.[4] On a reduced and inverted scale, the mechanism was in a sense similar to the one engineered by Luigi Einaudi in favor of large Italian firms and intelligently "unveiled" by Hirschman during the Marshall Plan (Hirschman, 1948).

The main difference, of course, was that the redirection of southern manufacturing activities was in reverse (from medium-sized to small activities) and was not planned at all—it was spontaneous and unexpected. Indeed, it was not even desired—either by the central government, nor the notables who controlled the southern political system, nor even by the main business associations, dominated as they were by medium and

---

2 From Meldolesi (2022), *Protagonismi mediterranei*: 26-30.
3 Especially with reference to the so-called "Third Italy." Why should the possibility be ruled out a priori that the productivity development in the North and Center whose beginnings had included even semi-submerged enterprises could be repeated (*mutatis mutandis*) in the South as well?
4 Attracting and productively setting in motion capacities and resources that had been expelled or initially dispersed, latent or badly utilized.

large companies. This was because, in favoring the countryside and the suburbs over city centers, and unintentionally redistributing money and power in favor of the small-scale productive classes (small businessmen and workers) at the expense of both the traditionally predominant and welfare-recipient classes, it effectively threw the existing social order into turmoil. In other words, the mix of economic policies that had taken hold at the European and national levels (as a result of accelerated East German infrastructure and the budget—and legitimate management—crisis at the national level) had had unintended consequences in the Mezzogiorno that no one (whether in Brussels or Rome, or even locally) had foreseen.[5] At the same time, however, it created the prospect (and the hope) that such a lucky *ouverture* might in the end lead to a real rehabilitation and transformation of the Mezzogiorno. It was in that climate, in that "unexpected productive boom" of semi-regular SMEs (especially in the vast Neapolitan hinterland) that our own story was in fact set in motion.[6]

And we must also add to all this the emergence of hitherto almost unknown productive centers (or *vulcanelli*)—such as the "Atellano quadrilateral"[7] or S. Giuseppe Vesuviano, along with the desire for a leading role (and for revenge) on the part of the inhabitants of the *"contado"* with respect to the city of Naples.[8]

---

[5] This was probably an unexpected (but from a possibilist point of view, important) positive aspect of "not being thought of at all"—as they say in Naples. . .

[6] Unfortunately—as I made clear in Meldolesi 2000 [in "Mezzogiorno e Germania dell'Est" reprinted in Meldolesi (2022)]—our proposals for accelerating this process did not pass at the political level. On the contrary, the reverse process occurred. This was because the dampening of the German macroeconomic thrust on the one hand, and the famous Maastricht parameters imposed for our participation in the euro on the other (including the abolition of the taxation of social security contributions in the Mezzogiorno, which was unjustly considered "state aid"), together with domestic welfare pressures, sounded the general retreat—that is, they largely blocked and reversed the expansionary process that had been set in motion. It was the beginning of the (deflationary) era of so-called austerity....

[7] Named after the ancient city of Atella, with Grumo Nevano at its center.

[8] This was followed, with some delay, by the perception on the part of Naples' more

Other factors included the enthusiasm of the economics students at Federico II University,[9] whom I asked to survey the manufacturing situation in their home towns, as well as my past social experience, which led me to explore the territory on the ground, including through the families of undergraduates (and graduates). There was also the controversy over the surveys of employment statistics, and of course the major press campaigns, embarrassing to the country's technical establishment, that were unleashed by some journalist friends, etc.

In other words, due to motives that were partly spontaneous and partly provoked, a major social wave rose up. The issue of semi-legal businesses and work emerged *au grand jour*— and swept through the government. Nevertheless, despite all the efforts of my student collaborators and myself, the result was... *thumbs down!*

The government, which boasted of being the first from the left since Garibaldi's time, did not lift a finger to encourage and regularize the widespread development taking place in the Mezzogiorno. And it thereby forced the dissolution of the great collective process involving young people, corporations and semi-regular workers which, surprisingly, we had managed to set in motion.

Why? Due to a whole series of circumstances: ignorance in Rome as in Brussels of what was actually going on; negotiations over the introduction of the Euro which had no qualms about sacrificing the regularization of the Mezzogiorno on the altar of the single currency; "Northern" predominance in key

---

adventurous intellectuals of what was actually happening. This was thus an indirectly acquired "detection" which, as I mentioned in the case of my friend Nicolaus, allowed an articulation of the reasoning, yes, but certainly not a commitment in the field... *Noblesse oblige!*

[9] The faculty had recently been moved from the waterfront on Via Caracciolo to Monte S. Angelo. In a developing automobile-oriented society like that of the province of Campania, this fortunately favored young people from the hinterland (the mountains and plains) over those from the city.

government posts; open opposition from administrative personnel; ostracism by the CGIL, etc.

And yet, this was not the end of our story. The sympathy our struggle had raised in some intellectual, political, and trade union circles eventually led these latter to invent a small escape hatch. This was mainly thanks to Alberto Carzaniga (friend and advisor to Carlo Azeglio Ciampi, then Budget and Treasury Minister), Marco Biagi (advisor to Tiziano Treu, Minister of Labor), and Stefano Ruvolo, CISL confederation secretary of Sicilian origin, who was already involved in numerous corporate labor "realignment" contracts in Puglia. They were the ones, in fact (directly and/or indirectly) behind the Treu-Ciampi Commission that proposed to Parliament (which approved it) a piece of legislation—Law 448/98—establishing the National Committee and Local Commissions for the Emergence of Unregulated Labor.

But in the meantime, the overall situation had been getting murkier.[10] Nevertheless, when Nicola Rossi, on behalf of Massimo D'Alema, then Prime Minister, proposed that I become chairman of the National Committee for Emergence, I accepted (the only condition being that I be able to work on it full time and be relieved of my teaching duties in Naples). Because the issue was by now on everyone's lips, and I felt I could still be useful to the collective movement that I had miraculously managed to set in motion . . .

I had (and have) high regard for collective processes, which in a sense represent the "salt" of democracy and its evolution. In fact, by "shaking the tree," as it were, they put meaning into the shell of our democratic market-economy societies. They

---

[10] As early as the summer of 1996, Fiorella Kostoris Padoa-Schioppa, then president of Ispe, had graciously forwarded to me the Trend Forecasts on the Italian economy in the three-year period 1997-1999 from one of her hearings before the Chamber, which indeed indicated that a process of progressive slowdown had begun to show itself.

bring issues of paramount importance to public attention, and at the same time they undermine stratified balances of spatial and temporal subordination, opening up significant new avenues and facilitating renewal.

Luca Meldolesi

Opening lesson of the Course in "Economic Policy"
(a.y. 1994-95) 17 March 1995[11]

Discovering the Possible – The Surprising World of Albert Hirschman
(Meldolesi 1995) is the only book that currently exists on the
extraordinary experiences of this author, one of the greatest
economists and social scientists of the century, perhaps of all
time, whom Aleandro Diaz (South American economist) has
called "the Mozart of the social sciences."

From an early age Hirschman found and embarked on a
path toward the discovery of the possible, and if he eventually
assumed a role of such importance, it was because the discovery of the possible carried with it another very significant consequence—it made it easier for humans to make progress.
There is a social-political thesis, humanistic if you will, at the
heart of it all, and this is the noblest aspect of the social sciences. Economics, sociology, philosophy, geography, history
are constructed with ethical intent—that is, they must serve the
betterment of human life. There is an idea of internal progress—the discovery of the possible. According to this point
of view, invented by a brilliant Italian philosopher named Eugenio Colorni,[12] we realize in our experience that there are
things beyond what we immediately perceive, and through our
own research we can make them known to us and bring them
out into the open.

---

[11] From *Italia Vulcanica* 2 (2019)17-23.
[12] Hirschman dedicates a small statement to him in *Crossing Boundaries* (1998): "I
realized that Eugenio Colorni was the most important man in my life."

A Cultural Break

Colorni, living in an era of great falsehood, the era of Italian fascism, posited the idea of a cultural break as the key to the possibility of taking back our own country. Do not passively accept the thinking that has been handed down—make an effort to understand. Out of that came an enduring journey that reaches all the way down to us, spanning an entire era. In fact Colorni was a philosopher of the 1930s, and he and Hirschman were together in those years. Hirschman received his degree in Trieste, but after the war they never saw each other again. Colorni was killed by the Nazi-Fascists fifteen days before the liberation of Rome.

The problem for Colorni was to understand how things really are and to discover whether this understanding is immediately obvious. Basically, while we perceive a range of things, we have the problem of how to process them—so there is a theory that concerns the processing of immediate, perceived knowledge. Colorni says that if people had other senses, they would see reality in a different way. Psychological science has taught us in recent decades that we see, we perceive, the things we do because we are human. If we hear music, it is because we have ears. If we set aside the human element, this same music is simply a wave. For humans it is music, but abstracting from humans it is a wave propagated in a vacuum. The same is true for other sensations such as color. This is to say that when it comes to perception, the personal, individual aspect can never be completely eliminated.

So we find ourselves having to do human social sciences with a purpose, which is human civilization. Or in the highest sense, giving impetus to civilization, going in search of what is possible in order to create more possibilities, and thus to find ways out of the situation we find ourselves in. We must do it for people but also as people, bringing our subjective condition into the discussion.

Colorni says that there are various levels of consciousness, but that the one that counts is the one that "goes through you," and makes the question personal as well. Therefore, in setting out to gain knowledge it is not enough simply to try to understand the object, we also must study our own reactions to it—we must split in two and look at ourselves. This self-reflection is crucial, and it is essential not to be afraid of what we find. This is where the trouble starts. We have to go out in search of the possible with the noble purpose that is human civilization, trying to understand the object—our society, our economy, our Mezzogiorno. All this cannot be done objectively. It requires that we track our subjectivity, find ways of limiting it, and then make the most of this capability. Our life itself becomes a quest for the possible.

Let us now look at an example. We place ourselves as subjects in front of an object with the aim of trying to find out as much as we can about this object. We must position ourselves in relation to it so that we get as many inputs as we can. How do we do this? Colorni's answer is very simple: we must put ourselves in a receptive position with respect to the object. This may seem banal, but since we are humans and as such mix our own desires with the objects that we see, it is actually quite complex. To make progress in gaining knowledge, therefore, it is essential that we wage a no-holds-barred battle against the tendency to delude ourselves. If we are overwhelmed by illusions, we will eventually crash into reality and then go through a period of depression—and it is only after this that we will be reborn with many of our illusions dispelled. To avoid this we must maintain constant vigilance against our tendency to create illusions. We must strive to represent things in their stark reality, and only then can we place ourselves in a receptive relationship. This means that instead of imposing ourselves on the facts, we must have the intelligence to let the facts affect us.

What we need to do, that is, is to reverse our reasoning.

SURPRISE

The book's subtitle is *The Surprising World of Albert Hirschman*. Let us now look at the meaning of the word "surprising." If we are receptive, then—if we fight our tendency to preempt things and desire other things—and we approach the world and life in this way, every now and then we will be surprised. We had spontaneously been expecting certain things but found others. If we are surprised it is because what we have in mind is different from what we actually see. Surprise means that we have called into question ways of thinking that we have in our heads, or even that we have seen some completely new thing that does not conform to our ways of thinking. Therefore, either because these gradually constructed ways of thinking are contradicted by reality, or because they are deficient—incapable that is of providing insight or explaining new things, we have in either case achieved a breakthrough. This breakthrough lies precisely in the fact that reality is much richer than our mind predicts it to be.

So what emerges here is a general thesis, essential to a modern type of social science work which is not simply preconceived, is not based on postulates, and does not just create models, etc., but is instead a complex process consisting of the relationship between human beings and their reality. When we are faced with surprise, we have a gateway to a reality that was not contemplated in our former way of thinking. So we have to set out to understand reality using all the means at our disposal. In other words our perceptions, first of all, and then all our direct and indirect knowledge. But then what is important is how we, as people who have lived a particular life, are able to process this knowledge, really understand it, process it effectively, and as a result obtain results that are true.

The problem, precisely, is that we find ourselves dealing with many products of thought that are true up to a point. Specifically, I am referring to the exams you take in Econ I and II.

You will certainly have to take others, and you are therefore well aware of what lies ahead. You are in for a fairly mnemonic course consisting of diagrams, graphs, and equations, which is generally constructed using deductive processes. That is, certain assumptions are made, and from these assumptions certain models are constructed which lead to certain conclusions that are generally deductions drawn from the assumptions. This is the typical modus operandi of what we call ECONOMICS. Why use this term rather than POLITICAL ECONOMY? Because I make a distinction between "economics" and "political economy." "Political economy" is an old term that came into existence in the seventeenth and eighteenth centuries in Italy and France. Then, with Adam Smith and the so-called birth of "scientific economics," it was transformed into "economics." My own point of view is essentially closer to political economy than to economics. Which is to say that it makes no general sense to me to separate economics from politics, especially if we are referring to economic policymaking, where the political aspect carries weight of its own. I do not want to transform "economic policy" into a simple deduction from "economics." In my view the key feature of "economic policy" is politics. Therefore, in this course we will speak of economics and politics and many other things.

ECONOMIC POLICY

We will position ourselves towards "economics" mindful of its degree of partiality with respect to our subject matter, but at the same time we will keep in mind the concepts that come to us from "economics" (effective demand, preferences, etc.). In essence, we will be setting up a connecting bridge that allows us to use certain concepts and theories that are significant to the study we are going to undertake. In fact, our study follows a cognitive path that is not simply deductive, not a deduction from assumptions, but rather an interaction—that is, inductive and deductive at the same time. If I stand in relation to reality, I have to interact with it; I infer things from my mind but I also inductively absorb things from reality.

In the case of surprise, the impulse comes from reality, so it is first of all inductive—it is us noticing something new, something different from what we thought. So it is an induction. Then we think it over and we say: if this is the way things are…, it should also be the case that… And in this way we start offering hypotheses, we organize them, we create something coherent, and by means of deductive logic we come back once again to reality.

Now, as far as "economics" goes, we would not go so far as to say that there is no observation of reality whatsoever—clearly anyone who constructs a model must have had some sort of insight. The point is that in economics what counts after that is the model. So this starting observation is in a way abandoned to its fate, it's a random observation that crops up no telling how, just for the sake of making the models. And once the model is made you simply deliver it, without bothering to see what happens when you compare the model to reality. Now it should be obvious that from the standpoint of economic policy this type of approach is quite a serious matter. It is serious because considering that economic policy decisions concern millions of people, it seems clear that we should also look at what the consequences of certain actions actually are. Instead it is typical of economic studies to put certain models to work without any awareness of how approximate they are, and not bother about analyzing the effects or the outcome or about weighing them against the objectives. All this is extremely dangerous. Economists have been capable in the past of fomenting popular uprisings, economic crises, etc., precisely because they did not take responsibility for their own advice.

At this point we need to establish a new way of looking at economic policy. It must seek a relationship with vast masses of people, taking their behavior into account. It must try and persuade them to behave in ways that are compatible with the results it proposes to pursue, and it must create a true consensus in this pursuit. Without all this, economic policies can produce out and out disasters.

THE BRAZILIAN EXPERIENCE

The Brazilian experience is emblematic—we can see with our own eyes what happened when the reasoning came only from the standpoint of "economics" and when, on the contrary, an attempt was made to adhere to the structure we are explaining now.

The economists of the Collor presidency[13] were very traditional. When Zelia was economy minister, they devised a series of plans to fight inflation (which at the time was in three figures, fluctuating between 100% and 1000%, with very high peaks), and the plans they adopted were along the lines of "God help us." To make a long story short, this Zelia went so far as to freeze personal deposits, so that people (I'm referring to the middle class) suddenly found themselves without money, not knowing how they could buy goods and services. This resulted in a return to certain forms of bartering (one doctor told me that suddenly everyone was bringing him capons)—an incredible leap backwards. The shock that this brand of "economics" provoked in its attempt to block inflation was probably one of the causes of Cardoso's winning the office of the presidency[14]. (Cardoso is a sociologist and part of the international circle linked to Hirschman).

If we compare Cardoso's economic model with Collor's, the differences are not great, but there is nevertheless a huge divergence. The economic project constructed by the economists linked to Cardoso has gone through a certain process:

---

13 Fernando Collor de Mello was President of Brazil between 1992 and 1994.
14 Fernando Henrique Cardoso was President of Brazil between 1995 and 2003.

17

1) general discussion
2) explanation to the people of what was about to happen
3) creation of a vast consensus in support of the project.

This procedure yielded the desired results, with inflation falling from 1000% to 20% last year alone. All this, in a country as tormented as Brazil has been, is something truly extraordinary. The outcome led to Cardoso's election in the first round of balloting with 54% of the vote.

Eyewitnesses tell me that one of the most important effects was something we generally don't think about. And why don't we? Because we don't have a true sense of how things actually work. We do not investigate. We don't do concrete, reality-based research. In Brazil, during a period of very high inflation, the poorest people, without access to banks either for deposits or credit, suffered greatly from the inability to save and thus to buy even the simplest items for their homes. As soon as prices stabilized people gained the ability to save something each month (which had not been possible previously because their savings would have been eaten up by inflation). And lo and behold, suddenly last year Brazil had a boom in home appliances. All the Brazilian *favelas*, this huge population somehow squatting on the fringes of modern civilization (amounting to 30 or 40 percent of the Brazilian population)—all these people have rediscovered the pleasure of being able to improve their own specific material conditions.

This goes to show how an economic policy built from a Hirschmanian point of view—that is, integrating different types of knowledge (psychology, sociology, economics, history) for the sake of a higher collective interest, can create a path enabling an objectively suffering population to take a step forward. No one can guarantee that the road will remain open after that, but it is nonetheless an interesting example because it allows us to see the big difference between "economics" and the Hirschmanian concept of "economic policy."

FOR A PRACTICAL AND DEMOCRATIC ECONOMIC POLICY

In conclusion, the idea that emerges from the books you have studied is that there are certain people who miraculously, we don't quite understand how, independently of anyone else, with no relationship with others, create a Science (capital S) from which precepts are drawn that are meant to apply to everyone. Thus, there is a recurring temptation, a serious danger to democracy, to use these precepts as leverage to impose certain behavior on everyone. This can be done from the RIGHT, but it can also come from the LEFT. So that we find, both on the right and the left, an intransigent position that claims to be right because "their model proves it." And then, basically, the leverage is applied to all of us. The problem we have—myself, Albert Hirschman, and a few others—is to get beyond this somewhat rudimentary stage of setting up the elements of civilized living, and to actually enter into a more deeply democratic relationship. Therefore, my "economic policy" I would say is PRACTICAL (as opposed to abstract) AND DEMOCRATIC, because it must never lose sight of the conditions and problems of the people.

PART II

Teaching and Organization

Luca Meldolesi

My Idea about Slack[1]

(.....) A number of times, especially in supervising theses slated
to become "super theses," I have happened to discover that a
candidate has remarkable capabilities that he or she is not actually aware of. In cases where such people are at the point of
giving up, I manage to convince them that this would be sui-
cide—just like jumping out the window. I pick them up by the
hair, work out with them an escape route for transforming the
thesis, calm them down, motivate them, and then, with Nicoletta's critical contribution, launch them toward the goal.
This is the way it was with Laura, Tito, Paolo—and now with
Mita. By extension (because their stories are more complicated)
this was also true in the cases of Gianni, Maurizio, Stefania,
young Nicoletta, etc. All of them needed to get through a bottleneck, through a narrow canyon that at first sight looked im-
passable but then suddenly opened out into the grasslands.

I became an expert at these kinds of acrobatics. "The doctor is in," says Nicoletta with affectionate irony. You have to
catch the person at the right moment—in some difficult situation or crisis that comes out in the open, revealing limitations
and potentials at the same time. You have to be able to motivate their will and support them in their efforts to surmount
the obstacle they are facing. When a breakthrough exercise like
this succeeds, the consequences are significant and lasting.

Despite the ups and downs (both during recovery and
later), the subject will not forget the experience and will be able
to draw on his or her recently tested ability and force another
breakthrough. While such incidents are probably numerous in

---

[1] From Meldolesi (2020), *Eppur si può*: 210-222.

each of our lives, some are more important than others—they represent a *denouément*, they raise awareness and can thus shed light on many other cases (our own as well as others'). Once the false bottom of the suitcase (or false lid, as Albert says) is opened, subjects are able to overcome the crisis. They improve their performance, enter a positive aspiration-achievement cycle, have a higher regard for their own abilities, and can live and work with greater satisfaction.

In my experience, this "cure" is easier if the tension is neither too high (as in social struggles), nor too low. And when there is a genuine need for redemption. This is in fact the condition of the Mezzogiorno. Here subjects have a desire to progress, but they imagine such a thing as a great leap that will in practice prove impossible. The truth is that they are held back by fear of what lies ahead. It is a contradictory condition that can only be overcome by letting tempers cool, separating (as much as possible) reality from desire, dividing the path into successive steps, and carefully studying variants and pathways. But once the way is clear and one's own capabilities are unleashed, the subject becomes immersed in a world that *ex ante* seemed improbable but then proves possible. He or she begins to gain confidence in expanding and exploring this dimension.

This "extra gear" is very valuable. I think I stumbled upon it initially as a combined effect of a hard initiation (my education at Cambridge, UK) and a movement of rebellion (in the 1960s). It was this antagonism that ignited the first spark because it convinced me that in order to walk my own path, I would have to "force" myself to make full use of what I was capable of doing. Logically, I transferred this viewpoint first to the social movements and then to my teaching in Rome in the 1970s. Even then, my thesis writers had to make their way across a course of trenches, and those who succeeded found that they had now unwittingly made a high investment in their own abilities. Moreover, as I got closer to Albert Hirschman, this inclination I had was gradually refined and regenerated, to the point of facilitating the birth of our subsequent experience. Now I think I need to theorize it in order to go further—to try and turn our association into a "collective miracle" and to start it "spilling over" into politics and production.

We will talk more about politics. For now, I will only mention that Maurizio Maturo (mayor of Mugnano di Napoli) has set out along this road at a fast pace; while I, mindful of past difficulties, believe that an exploit of this kind first and foremost requires that we strengthen our "internal forum," whose research dimension makes it particularly suitable for rigorous initiation and personal emancipation. Under such conditions, the passion for change almost begins to look like a self-fulfilling prophecy. This can produce, as Maurizio has shown, significant external fall out, and it can also represent, when needed, a seedbed of scientific support.

I come finally to a more personal matter. The satisfactory results, in Italy and abroad, of my work have undoubtedly given me confidence—for some time now I seem to have improved in my acrobatic exercises. But I still have much to learn. Stefania S. says I am a constant. This is not true, or ought not to be, although I may have given that impression. I find it easier to use voice than exit, to speak rather than to be silent. For one thing, I feel too responsible for what happens around me.

These are imperfections, yet they weigh me down because I don't feel like I can move as I want to. And as I should. Because you have to be on the alert to notice opportunities, and then you have to take them in order to savor them, understand them, and decide accordingly.

The idea of slack generally refers to known capabilities and resources. But others exist that are hidden because they are unknown—even to those who possess them.[2] This procedure has

---

2 Eugenio Colomi, I think, would have approved. Albert knows this very well but does not say it. Perhaps he wants to avoid getting entangled. In any case he uses

endless variations, but in reproducing it one learns to master it gradually, to the point of harnessing the energy that can then be released at moments of adversity and crisis.

Finally, possibilities for improvement are reproduced when we are able to listen to each other carefully and evaluate our actions with a cool head. In this process, then, the concrete, almost tactile perception that one could do better becomes decisive. Perhaps, this is the most important thing Albert Hirschman taught me. Fortunately, in studying his work, I have often felt a little stupid.

Comments 2019
Social energy and "the art of staying together"

1. Everyone's energy fluctuates, varying over time on a daily basis. We all have good days when we miraculously manage to get a lot of things done—more than we had planned. But we also have the bad day, when we are exhausted, when we have no edge.

Speaking of which, where does the vitality and vigor go in such cases? Must it be hiding somewhere? The following pages attempt to unravel this 'mystery' to some extent. And to clarify my line of reasoning as much as possible, I will assume that while the capabilities and resources of each of us (humans) are often very different from those of others, their total energy can always be divided into two parts: the energy we use every day and a 'surplus' that instead appears and disappears depending on the conditions.

In other words, we all possess an undercurrent of energy

---

subtle and very personal unblocking techniques quite different from those mentioned above.

that can be mobilized, even though we often do not even realize it.[3]

In Albert Hirschman's work, we see this potential, for example, in the *Hiding Hand* (Hirschman, 1967)—hiding, that is, difficulties in development projects that can be overcome if the subject is able to activate (in quality and quantity) his or her dormant creative vein. Or in *The Principle of Conservation and Mutation of Social Energy* (Hirschman, 1984) —a concept that implies the pre-existence of a store of additional energy, some of which has fortunately been saved (rather than dissipated) and can once again be activated in a different form.

So this "surplus" of energy actually exists—even if we have yet to understand how it comes into the world and concretely manifests itself. In the two texts mentioned—and again in *The Changing Tolerance* [or *Tunnel Effect*] (Hirschman 1973) and in *Shifting Involvements* (Hirschman 1982)—there is a human need linked to some dissatisfaction (private or public) that plays the role, so to speak, of midwife, pushing subjects to overcome their natural tendency to "save their energy," and thus to expend the effort needed to mobilize their surplus energy.

But this (obviously) in no way rules out the possibility that the impetus for the release of dormant energy may occur on the positive side of the equation[4]—for example, through the influence of a particularly persuasive lecturer, a passion that suddenly appears, a sporting event, etc.

---

[3] But once brought into focus, we find it everywhere. We need only close our eyes and think of the different stages of human life—from the exuberant children who spontaneously harness their energies in play to young people who learn to gradually measure out the "strengths" they possess; from those who become accustomed to a low-voltage life (often unaware of its consequences), to the elderly who, up to a certain point, can compensate with quality for their inevitable "energy reduction."

[4] As for example in the case of Greta Thunberg. In effect, under certain conditions a young person who unintentionally had a slow or uncertain start can suddenly come out of the woodwork, giving free rein to his or her extraordinary energy...

It is an issue too closely linked to the training and education of young people not to suggest that it should be reintroduced, *mutatis mutandis*, in the school environment. The "lazy"
student is, by definition, someone who could do better than he
or she actually does—that is, who "couldn't care less" about
dispensing the required effort. The consequence is that he or
she (generally) has a rather modest level of self-esteem—feeling, more than others, "inadequate" with respect to life's ne-
cessities.

By contrast, those who do make an effort follow the opposite logic and (sometimes) realize that they can bring to bear
capabilities and resources that until then they thought were not
even within their reach. This kind of "discovery" may thus spur
them to increase their efforts still further. [5] Collective movements imply a trajectory that in its initial exuberant stages generally follows such logic.

2. On the other hand, it is well known that Eugenio Colorni (six years older than Albert Hirschman), who felt the full
weight of responsibility of the era of "steel and fire" (the
1930s-40s), had great respect for psychology and psychoanalysis, which he considered even more important for the healthy
than for the sick. He believed that a part of our subconscious
could be decoded, mastered, and put to work (for noble ends,
of course).

---

[5] Here a problem within a problem comes to the surface. Because compared to
others, the person who learns to get mobilized undoubtedly enjoys a notable relative
advantage. This allows such a person to make commitments in many different
directions. And this may come into conflict with the need (equally crucial) to impose
a system of priorities on his or her life (which must in turn be dealt with in a certain
established order). It then becomes critical to learn how to reconcile such "primary
needs," so to speak. On one hand, without self-mobilization the energy is often
insufficient with respect to the goal. While on the other, without self-discipline the
energy is dissipated and thus no longer can generate real momentum or lead to the
expected outcome. Naturally, the multiplicity of goals in real life makes the pattern
even more complex. Nevertheless, the point still stands.

In this regard there existed without a doubt a certain difference between Eugenio and Albert. So much so that Hirschman—I now recall—told me at one point that he had teased Colorni by challenging him with, "[...] all right, supposing I did have an Oedipus complex: how would you tell?" And (I would argue) the latter did not know what to say in return.

In this "tempest in a teapot" something deeper can probably be discerned. In fact, it is clear that because of his natural reticence, his stateless condition (with an FBI "file" hanging over his head), and the individualistic American environment he lived in (where, for reasons of privacy, no one is allowed to intrude in the affairs of others), Albert never got past a certain "insuperable barrier"—regarding both himself and (above all) his students.

For Eugenio, on the other hand, things were different. He would test on himself and his environment any changes in energy that might occur. He left us a wonderful essay on his teaching in Trieste along with three extraordinarily significant autobiographical pieces.[6]

And in addition, even if we are not able to document it completely, it is clear that his work with the young socialist federalist in Nazi-occupied Rome in 1943-1944 had a very advanced capacity for Socratic discourse, especially when it came to bringing out and properly cultivating surplus energy—his own and that of others.

3. *Rebus sic stantibus*, it seems to me that the experience (of the last 35 years!) that I have built up with so many young collaborators is again something different. The reasons are as follows:

---

[6] See "The Function of the Teacher in the Fascist School" in Colorni (2019) and "Beginning an Autobiography", "Justification" and "The Philosophical Illness" in Colorni (2021).

a) The release of potential energy on the part of Liliana Bac-ulo's students and mine happened during their formative phase—they discovered early on that they were different from the way they had thought of themselves before.

b) Even from within inevitable processes of oscillation, my efforts were always directed toward keeping the use of in-dividual and collective surplus energies (including mine and Nicoletta Stame's, of course) at a high level, and to direct them appropriately (while inviting each person to make free use of very wide margins of discretion). This was possible thanks to the decade of Roman rebellion we had behind us (1968-1977)[7] and because, by possibilist means, we worked tirelessly to identify opportunities for stimulating players—local, national and international.

c) In this way, the battle against isolation, "the art of staying together" (which we have uniquely inspired over so many years), along with the many development projects we have undertaken, have allowed us, as a "network," to sustain an average energy level much higher than others—this is what we normally call our (peculiar) vitality.

d) Furthermore, even through all the ups and downs, applied possibilism, as a tool for recognizing opportunities and intervening *in corpore vili*, has maintained our close (and of-ten confidential) level of focus on "our own business" and its actual results (and thus on the significance of the poli-cies pursued). Our obsession with results "*ha fatt'a grazia*"! [has brought grace]

e) Finally, when the process truly got under way (as in 1994-1996), it had an energizing effect on the surrounding am-bience in the sense that it offered future prospects and acted as a driving force "[…] carrying everyone with it." That is, it suggested to a wider circle of acquaintances, friends, co-workers, fellow travelers, etc., that they could

---

[7] It's true—I would never have been able to promote the small Neapolitan young people's surge of 1994-1996 (and then inspire and support some important consequences) if Nicoletta and I had not had that experience.

call on their surplus energy and "do the right thing."[8]

4. Conclusion: precisely because we ourselves have had this experience, we have always given participants the opportunity to transfer it and reproduce it *mutatis mutandis* (trespassing) in any field—in their workplace first and foremost (and thus in businesses, cooperatives, public agencies, government, teaching, hospitals, etc.).

Of course, it was not easy to "keep up the pace" of our work.[9] Many people watched from the outside. Quite a few participated in a specific phase (and remained attached to a specific but indelible memory of it), while still others lost contact, and perhaps, later, found it again, etc.

---

[8] I only now realize that in doing so I have not taken the path marked out by Eugenio. I did not have a "great respect for psychology and psychoanalysis"; I did not commit myself to studying them as disciplines; I did not read the classic texts of the main protagonists of those sciences; I did not try to decode parts of my subconscious in order to master it; I did not write autobiographical texts, etc. Why? Probably because, while coming to terms with my previous theoretical consciousness (concerning economics; and Marxism), I never lost sight, over many years, of Albert's example. Because since the 1980s (and thus since the beginning of the present adventure) I have taken possession of possibilism and applied it in an 'extensive' way, for political (and economic policy) reasons, to my teaching, to the training of my students, in local projects, etc. Because the good results thus achieved convinced me that for my own purposes, a real investment in the sciences of the psyche was not indispensable—I could fend for myself. Only later did we feel a growing need to understand Colorni better...

[9] Not because there were many who lacked the desire to do so. But because the difficulty of untangling the meanderings of their own evolution suggested to them different ways of handling the relationship between energy mobilization, self-discipline, and the ends to be achieved (see, n. 5 above). It was therefore a more or less conscious "life choice, freely made." One example should suffice. Of the 15 students and friends immortalized in a famous historical photo with Albert in Naples at Liliana Baculo's house, only three are still working with Nicoletta and me in the Coloni-Hirschman Institute. Yet, that those three are actually there to "faticare appresso" [toil side by side] (as they say in Neapolitan) with others is undoubtedly decisive, not least for reasons of historical memory—in showing the surprising continuity, vitality, and possible rebellions that have again and again been renewed in our experience.

It is true in general that only a very few were able independently to get the things they had learned to flourish elsewhere. For most, "losing touch" (as they often put it) also meant a return to normalcy and thus a relapse into "neglecting" much of their surplus energy.

This helps explain for example why the demise of social movements produces a memory that oscillates between a good experience and a waste of time.

For us this was not the case. Our season, with its thousand ups and downs (and with the entrances and exits of numerous protagonists), has managed to endure, and now occupies an important space in our lives—demonstrating, moreover, the need to further develop the Colornian-Hirschmanian arsenal we have learned to utilize.[10]

The fact is, our conception of slack goes beyond Albert's idea of abilities and resources that are "hidden, scattered, or badly utilized" (the paradigm that he claimed to have hatched over time with a distinguished group of thinkers. Hirschman 1984; now in 1986, pp. 12-14)

Because everyone, I say every human being, has a surplus of energy that can be appropriately harnessed.[11] And there are

---

[10] In fact, to return to the argument in n. 5, I want to add that while generally speaking it is movements that lend credence to goals, in the specifics of the interrelationship between the pursuit of goals and the mobilization of energies, the former often acted as the driving force behind the latter (in the sense that the person was persuaded to make a commitment to "becoming capable" and thereby even more useful to everyone). Only now, in order to become collectively capable of tackling a goal as highly improbable as the creation of a worldwide "network," I felt the need to reverse that relationship for the purpose of asking myself (ourselves) what it is that hinders, holds back our enterprise as regards a shared goal such as the very ambitious one just mentioned. So it was enjoyable, through Viviana F.'s inquisitive willingness, to initiate a small individual psychological exploration that will allow us to inquire into the matter without delay.

[11] And consequently, there is no person in the world who cannot be beneficially employed. Concerning healthy people, Gennaro di Cello recently reminded me of my idea, adding that thanks to my suggestion he successfully brought about the transformation of a particularly inept young person into a solid pillar for a collective

many people (the elderly above all) who, paradoxically, just do not know what to do with their lives. To the extent that if I had to say whether there was more slack or non-slack in the world around us, I wouldn't be able to answer.

On the other hand, I had put the "affective method"—as the primary system for consciously activating and orienting people and things—into practice independently long before I became aware of Eugenio's insights on love (Colorni 2019: 83-92). And also long before I discovered in a 1995 letter from Albert a special interest he had in "competent rebels"—which evidently excludes both incompetent rebels and the many competent people... who are not rebels (Meldolesi ed. 2019b).

5. Essentially, it is a matter of carefully exploring the ulterior consequences of our innovations. They are, at one and the same time, crucial correlates of our approach and important tools that enable the approach to reveal itself as it is—an effective part of life as it is lived.

For example, take the 1959 letter to Chenery that Albert had forgotten (and I reminded him of – Meldolesi 1995: 63) where he wrote that in *The Strategy* his "main assumption is that underdeveloped economies are *squeezable.*" Well, from our experience we can (obviously) confirm this thesis. But we don't stop there.[12]

In fact, we have become virtuosos when it comes to "self-squeezing"—that is, day-to-day behavior that in fact reconciles Hirschman's point of view with Colorni's while at the same time jointly displaying them both.

For many of us, in fact, it has become habitual to incrementally squeeze ourselves "just a little bit more"—enough to

---

venture they are putting together. In addition, for the disabled, we inaugurated in Berlin an exchange of "Basagliesque" experiences between Italian and German social cooperatives as a result of the Third Conference on Albert Hirschman's Legacy.

[12] I thank Roberto Celentano for suggesting that I make the following point explicit apertis verbis.

produce the desired breakthrough (which, up to that point seemed out of reach). It is a mindset that is not optimistic (which I am sometimes accused of being). It is simply encouraging (by design!), for me and for my listeners, whatever the situation. Because it is true to say that this latter can (and must) be improved—in every case…

In this way both the key thesis of "and yet you can" (the good news we broadcast left and right all over the world, and which is becoming our quasi-Galilean calling card), and its implementation in a hundred different situations have *ipso facto* become instruments for the multiplication (and encouraged utilization) of dormant energies…

Throw all this away?

"It would be a crime!" says Tommaso d. N., and I agree, I agree…

But we have to find a way to prevent such a crime; and also, to intelligently tackle the uphill climb in front of us.

Luca Meldolesi

On the Affective Method[13]

Rome, 27 May 1995

I would like my friends and students to remember three things about me. That I gave my all; that I tried, as an intellectual, to be militant, useful and free (I mean completely free). And that I taught using the affective method. I borrowed its current formulation from Eugenio Colorni, but I certainly practiced it—the affective method—long before I met Albert Hirschman.

Many people remember Nicoletta and Luca for this very reason. It used to be said: "to save the patient, fight the disease," and the emphasis was on the latter. What interested me, though, (and still does) was the former—after all, I am a doctor's son. Indeed, I believe it is possible to fight a disease effectively—and thus make inroads into others' beliefs—only if the overt intention is precisely to save the sick person. In other words, the other person needs to feel that I am trying to put myself in their shoes and see things from their point of view; that I am doing everything I can to help, lend support, open up new perspectives, etc. This affective outreach (at once useful and imaginative) cannot leave anyone unmoved.

Sometimes it is the first step in an actual "unblocking." More or less consciously, the person before us is searching for the key to their own problem. They have conscious orientations that do not fit with a deep need for personal emancipation.

Entering into a deep emotional relationship which at the

---

13 From Meldolesi (2020), *Eppur si può*: 233-235 and 237-241.

35

same time supports the need for change allows the person to see and understand something new, however confusedly, and to acquire an increased degree of self-understanding. This leads to a perception of possibilities opening up. The person feels reassured, encouraged and valued, to the point of finding the strength to act. They will discover a sense of liberation, of openness to "unexplored spaces," normally followed by a level of enthusiasm that may lead to a sort of infatuation. But if this can be restrained and kept within reasonable dimensions, it can in the end lead to serene resourcefulness. The subject will begin to identify with the affective method—with loving oneself.

The affective method is based on the principle of "giving in order to receive." The strength of its impact is in the notion of generosity—we are not used to others caring about our business, and some will take it for paternalism. But the simple fact that such an interest exists surprises us, and if it then leads to a positive outcome, we cannot help but feel gratitude towards whoever has brought it about. In this way, the initial generosity receives the gratitude of the recipient as an affective return.

This is where I get involved. The need I have to feel your emotional concern is related to another need—to see my own progress reflected in yours. Basically, you are my ambassadors. If it is clear that you are doing well, improving, discovering new abilities and perspectives, and asserting yourselves in a clean and righteous way, then I am happy for you, because you have more than earned it (and despite everything there is at least some justice in this world!). But I am happy for myself as well, because you represent the living proof that tropical flowers can bloom even and especially under difficult conditions. This is a success to be truly treasured. My untiring need to rise and to see that you do too, to improve the quality of the work—perhaps following different routes—this flows into a desire for its flowering. We are truly useful (to ourselves, to others, to the Mezzogiorno) only when we become truly "capable."

CONCLUSION. It is just as wrong only to give (altruism) as it is only to receive (selfishness)—both the one and the other will lead us astray. Rather, our path climbs up through the vast mountainous terrain that exists between the two. The affective method teaches how to give in order to receive. Those who don't know how to practice it need to learn it. It must be made clear to them in every possible way, even to the point where relations break down, that they cannot expect to receive unless they learn to give—to give more than they receive. Only then, miraculously, will what they receive be enough.

Luca Meldolesi

A Magical Divide[14]

Tarquinia, 18 November 1999
Dedicated to Daniela Caianiello

Albert Hirschman doesn't just write extraordinary texts; he also devises projects that he later decides not to pursue. One of these comes to mind, probably because it helps clarify our own experience. It concerns the application of exit and voice to medieval history—specifically to the wanderings of Dante Alighieri. He mentioned it to me after having written his wonderful essay on the fate of the German Democratic Republic (GDR), as if he wanted to continue along the same line of reasoning.

Albert is a man of few words, and I don't actually know what he intended to write. But I can try to imagine. He probably wanted to go back to the topic to show that Stein Rokkan's reasoning about the concurrent repression of exit and voice in the medieval construction of European principalities might have a positive rebuttal.

At issue is the link between exit and voice. Normally exit weakens voice (the hydraulic model in *Exit*). Situations exist, however, in which exit enhances voice, or conversely, in which the suppression of exit muffles voice. Rokkan had argued against this reinforcing effect after the publication of *Exit*, and Albert had returned to it here and there in passing, mainly positively.[15] Finally he found a great opportunity to support it as a negative and (especially!) positive general thesis in the case of

---

[14] From Meldolesi, (2020) *Eppur si può*; p. 243-6.
[15] Cf. Meldolesi 1995, ch. 6, pp. 154-155 and ch. 7, pp. 165 and ff.

the GDR. Knowing him, it seems logical to me that what he wanted to do was to generalize the thesis in a broader historical context.

It may be that the undertaking appeared too challenging to him. In any case, three years ago (I think it was)[16] he flirted with the idea for several months and spoke to me about Dante Alighieri's wanderings among various Italian principalities. So when I encounter a plaque commemorating the great poet's passage through this or that district, I can't help rethinking the question and daydreaming about it. It would appear that the writing of the *Divine Comedy* and the very birth of Italian culture are linked to mutually reinforcing processes of exit and voice. In order to write his verses Dante needed the sort of freedom of thought that only exit could grant him. Perhaps, when things were going badly, he would find a way to leave—to recapture the peace he found in his work and revive his own free voice by changing districts. Perhaps this was how he managed to write his many horrifying stories about the powerful people of his time. Who doesn't remember Count Ugolino, with "his mouth uplifted from his grim repast"?

Dante's exit from Florence was certainly not a detachment, a final separation. On the contrary, it served to build and express what he truly intended to stand for. In short—I am still imagining—Dante was casting about for that "fusion point" between exit and voice that produced the miracle of his poetry.

An interesting idea? Possibly. Maybe when the people in our department think of a trip as breath of fresh air this is what they mean. When we ourselves travel in Italy and abroad we are looking for something like this. When Laura T. says that in Cambridge, Mass. she felt as if she had emerged from a dark closet, this is exactly what she is talking about. When my students from small villages speak enthusiastically about the

---

16 Therefore in 1996.

course, they mean to say that the course is a useful counterpoint to local life.

In short, the idea is that there is this sensitive point, a special and almost contiguous interval in the exit-voice relationship. We must seek this and set it in motion because it powerfully activates a recovery mechanism within us, reducing our implosive tendencies, draining away the slack and increasing our productivity. It gives us more confidence, makes us less fearful, and encourages us to think and act. It helps us put our passion for change into practice.

So how do we identify this *punctum gaudens*? We know that a credible threat of exit activates voice, and that exit aimed at voice is then a powerful stimulus to our strength (and freedom) of expression. This means that on either side of this divide things are different.

In fact, if exit becomes the *Barber of Seville's* eternal refrain (*zitti, zitti, piano piano*...) no one will believe it, not even the Barber. Similarly, if by exiting we mean to turn our backs on our reality, we will at the same time be trying to drive it out of our minds: our inner voice will simply fail.

We can repeat this line of reasoning, but this time doubling the subjects of the exit-voice relationship. If no one exits no one speaks, but if it is the most active who exit, those left behind will no longer speak. This is why I still think that my coming and going between Rome and Naples (and the world outside) is the best solution for me and for you.

For me because it allows me to activate multiple convergent recovery mechanisms. For you because you receive a great many inputs and at the same time you are free (indeed totally free) to act for the best. This is the secret of my "towing with headway" as Paolone called it. It is a tow that stops in one place and picks up in another, and vice versa. It is oxygen that is invigorating only when used independently, as an actual recovery. It's like when the lights come on—but only for the time it takes to go up the stairs. Then you have to take action yourself to turn the switch back on. And it's not always easy.

We all have to learn to activate these recovery mechanisms. We need to fight any sort of depression. Get right back into shape in the contacts among ourselves—contacts that are in fact composed of exit and voice, and are strengthened by intelligent allegiance to the pursuit of common goals.

Comments 2019
High Tides

1. Even in its autonomous expression, it is true that thought mirrors (and reflects) experience—while relentlessly using past ideas, both one's own and others' (and vice versa). It thus happened that bringing the ideas of Albert Hirschman and his "circle" into contact with the real world in my Neapolitan work of the 1980s and 1990s logically enough suggested further insights—some published, some in the process of publication—which I intend to revisit.

It is therefore worthwhile (inspired by that author's famous "propensity for self-subversion") to gain a first-hand understanding, by means of an example, of the mental process by which such a development can unfold, incrementally and with contradictions.

It is well known that the ultimate roots of *Exit, Voice, and Loyalty* (Hirschman, 1970) are to be found in the "narrow tolerance for poor performance" inferred from the observation of Colombian airlines—the cornerstone on which Hirschman began to build *The Strategy of Economic Development* (Hirschman, 1958). Yet later, observing the Nigerian railways during the research that led him to *Development Projects Observed* (Hirschman, 1967) Albert realized that the exit from the trains (by motorists) could actually mute the voice (of railroad customers). And this was the source of the miracle of thinking (that creation of a something out of nothing) that gave birth to *Exit*…

Exit is an unplanned little volume, child of a "highly disputatious" era, which sparked a huge debate. In this way it involved multiple areas of American and international culture, and thereby moved forward in the actual construction of its own theoretical framework. Nevertheless, in the preface to the German edition of that work, Hirschman made it clear that the book's dominant relationship, in which exit muffles voice, likely reflects his own guilt (however irrational it may be) for abandoning the Jewish community in Berlin shortly after the advent of Hitler.

On the other hand, in his noted article "Exit, Voice, and the Fate of the German Democratic Republic" (now in Hirschman 1995), Albert maintained that the experience of the fall of the Berlin Wall (and more generally of the extraordinary social motion that led to the progressive enfranchisement of Eastern Europeans) enriched his theory by showing in concrete terms that exit can strengthen voice rather than weakening or stifling it.

2. At this point I have to confess that there is something in this long and winding journey that does not sit well with me. Why, I wondered, did Hirschman take so long to get to this final result, despite the countless appeals for it that he had received?[17] My answer would be that probably his concrete personal experience had not compelled him to seize it before this.[18]

17For example, having been set on the right track (from the negative side of this reinforcing relationship) by Stein Rokkan's work on the Medieval period (1974, 1975): cf. Hirschman 1974, 1976.

18With the exception, probably, of the little high tide he was part of during the almost two years (winter 1936-summer 1938) he spent in Trieste with Eugenio and Ursula. On the one hand Albert never recognized it as such. On the other, however, he spoke of it on several occasions (and even wrote about it) as a happy time in which, partly because of Eugenio, he was able for the first time to "get into gear"—

In fact, the youthful antifascist activities in Italy and France that he was so proud of (to the point of putting them ahead of his intellectual work in terms of importance; Coser 1984) "preceded" the popular high tide of 1943-1945, while after this he in effect did not participate in the explosion of 1968 against the Vietnam war, partly because—as he told me[19]—he was busy in California (at Stanford's Center for Advanced Studies in Behavioral Sciences)... writing *Exit*.

Hence, then, the certain "divine surprise" that can be glimpsed in "Exit, Voice and the Fate of the German Democratic Republic," and even the cautious, though good humored and participatory attitude in the fall of 1994, if I remember correctly, when he concluded the course of international seminars organized at the high tide of my Neapolitan teaching career.[20]

3. So the question of exit and voice mutually reinforcing (rather than opposing) one another presented itself several times in the post-World War II period—with its peculiar impetuosity, but also with the raft of problems it brought with it from one time to the next, a subject that undoubtedly deserves more in-depth observation and study.

In *Shifting Involvements* (Hirschman, 1982) as well—and particularly in his well-known disagreement with Mancur Olson (1965) on *The Logic of Collective Action*—Albert attaches great importance to social movements because of their innovative drive and the ripple effects they produce "out through the branches" of society; but when it comes to high tides his perception does not seem so clear. That is to say, when there is

---

thus letting some key features of it shine through from his point of view. These are important elements of field observation that should be compared with similar ones observable from Eugenio and Ursula"s side (Meldolesi 2013 and 2019).

19In one of his typical "half-truths": cf. Hirschman 1968, pp. 4-5.

20In other words, it can perhaps be argued that in fact this issue had appeared "under the radar" several times in Albert's career, that he found a way to bring it to the surface *apertis verbis* only in the case of the fate of the GDR, and that now, precisely because of this, it can be generalized cautiously—at both a large and small scale.

within a short period of time an ex ante unprecedented collective event that draws enormous attention and actually amounts to a verdict reached in the field, a break in continuity that later prevents a return to the starting point.

And what is more, Hirschman argued later that social conflicts are pillars of democratic market societies because they leave behind a valuable residue that facilitates their integration (so much so that our societies need "a steady diet of conflict"). But he does not even mention the high tides that powerfully multiply such processes—to the point that the subsequent "treatment" of their residue has major multiple consequences for entire generations…

4. On the other hand, it is also true that such a "collective upheaval" (so to speak) can also occur in reverse, when a long standing situation of apparently "permanent belligerence" suddenly dissolves and leaves the warring parties in the field united by the feeling that an entire phase has come to an end; and that it is time to return, somehow, to normality.

In fact, it is with these ideas in mind that we should re-examine *Shifting Involvements*, the widely known monograph which, as I mentioned, provoked such a heated argument among Albert's friends that he chose to downgrade it to a *bildungsroman*, precisely because it corresponded to his own experience, but not (necessarily) that of others.

Well, the very idea of high and low tides (upswings and downswings) may well help us to revisit that text and dig deeper into the collective oscillations that, as history teaches, surely pervade our existence.

Luca Meldolesi

Making Affect Work[21]

Valeria wants me to be clearer about the affective method. As you know, this is one of the (few) theoretical points our experience is based on. But with a difference. In the cases of slack, exit and voice, or public and private interests we can always appeal to Albert's elaborations and limit ourselves to reinterpreting them *pro domo nostra* (perhaps from a different perspective), for the affective method this is not the case. All we have is a penetrating insight of Eugenio's.

Yet the issue is central. It continually helps us to "register" each other's behavior and to consolidate our small structures. Remember when thesis groups fell apart at every turn? After Vincenzo's cure and then Valeria's and Nicola's, it doesn't happen anymore. It is truly extraordinary that today I can count on this solid rearguard. I just mentioned it to Joan Scott, a close friend of Albert and Sarah's who will be visiting us soon.

It is worthwhile, then, to offer a brief overview. In the first text on the affective method, from May 1995, I argued that the basis of this method (which respects and values the interlocutor by enjoying his or her difference) is the idea of giving in order to receive. At the end of last year, I think, I added that in doing this it is important to make sure that the beneficiary is aware of what is happening. He or she must be prevented from taking advantage of it, and must instead adopt an attitude of reciprocity, especially toward third parties. Now it occurs to me to add that this last observation stems from the fact that we are arranged on a scale by age and experience, and that the strength of the method therefore lies in how vigorously it can

---

[21] From *Italia Vulcanica*, n. 10 (2021): 55-56.

45

propagate from the top down.

It is this ripple effect that creates an environment of great satisfaction on the job that actually repays the actors, at different levels, for the effort of generosity that has been put forth. In this way then, affect induces affect and (by hook or by crook) drives away behavior that does not fit with it.

However, as our recent episode has shown, the affective method works well only in a world in which the other balances mentioned above are operating as well. For example: Daniela and Marco have made it to the home stretch (they have now won the battle against "our own slack"); Maurizio and Tommaso have found that (under certain conditions) their exit to Rome improves their voice locally; and in addition, Ignazio, Vincenzo, Sara, Valeria, Nicola, and Rosanna have also fortunately found a certain public-private balance. The combination of these ideas is the basis of our forward momentum. But sadly, the reverse is also true. A still-fragile construction, though accustomed to functioning under a thin skin, urgently needs concrete results. The work needs to grow—as Nicola rightly says.

Princeton NJ, 20 March

Luca Meldolesi
"Giving Everything" and Using Your Own Capabilities[22]

Dedicated to Daniela Caianiello

What you are saying among yourselves is that things are finally going well. For a while now I've been seeing attentive and intelligent faces around me, brightened by hope. Perhaps we have before us a constructive period of our now broad complex of Southern, Roman, Italian, and international activities. But if we really want this, we ought to reflect for a moment on why this was possible and how we can improve the outlook still further.

The potentials—clearly—were there. The "reform-monger," so your reasoning goes, sensed them and pursued them for a few months until they produced a surprising and heartfelt national reconciliation and a general sense of new momentum. Just so. But given that the "reform-monger" was me, I would like to let you know briefly what went on behind the scenes. When I took over the helm again before the summer, I became convinced that in order to harness the slim chances of success over a very broad horizon (three continents, a situation of domestic opportunities broken up into at least three parts—the South, Rome, and the North) I would have to start from the top and not lose sight of any of my best "cards." Albert has always been given priority in my work. Now, together with Albert and the US, we have added Brazil, without forgetting France (and Germany). I found that the resumption of this international work opened up new possibilities for me from above in Rome and Bologna. This is why I think the operation

---

[22] From *Italia Vulcanica* n. 2 (2019): 106-115.

should be repeated in the coming months: we need to revitalize the operation, not least so that we can make important progress here at home. The rest—Nomisma, Civil Service, 44, CNR, Artimino, etc.—came as a result (or was revitalized as a result), allowing our young people to breathe easier than before.

So it's true. Without our supranational strength we wouldn't have been able to get things back on track. And without its reactivation in the near future we won't be able to move our collective wagon forward. But only Luca knows how to do this—is what you'll be thinking. We can sit at home and wait for the roast pigeons. Get it out of your head.

Of course, I do not expect to turn you into international traveling salesmen. But I do expect each of you to a) properly understand how things are; b) reduce the number of mistakes you commonly make; and c) find ways to support—in appropriate ways—the process of change.

Firstly, in order to reactivate the blood flow of this venture of ours, I had to put all my energy into it. Every time I looked in the mirror, the dermatitis (which increases or decreases depending on my degree of anxiety) signaled to me whether I was succeeding (or not) in mastering the situation. And such mastery in turn allowed the resumption of "major works"—obviously the demonstration that our "dream" is achievable is a source of great satisfaction for me.

This was possible, clearly, because I decided to give "everything"—that is, to push my personal commitment both at home and abroad to the absolute limit, beyond which lies the beginning of material and mental decay. This "extremism" is in a sense inherent in my nature. I need to find out for myself whether what I have in mind can be written down (and if so, how), and above all whether it is feasible. I am an intellectual who needs to get things done. In short, seeing is believing—I might say with St. Thomas. And if I have to jump in in order to see, then I jump. Perhaps it is the transfer of my father's "experimental syndrome" to the social level. In any case, when I was younger, I was less aware of my limits and perhaps I came off badly. Now, though, I master myself better—body and soul—and I am able to push myself to the right point. The problem is that I have often hit that point in recent months and to push myself or be pushed beyond it would be counterproductive. This is a theme that deserves some developing.

Let us look at the argument in the way most congenial to you—from the bottom up. It is clear first of all that giving much to others is the basis of the affective method—a method based precisely on giving in order to receive. This year, with the adoption of *Discovering the Possible* (Meldolesi, 1995) alongside *Spender meglio è possibile* (Meldolesi, 1992) and with 450 students, I have exceeded all limits of quality and quantity. I promise myself a certain amount of downsizing. But still, with much effort I have managed to get on top of the situation. The (late) November exams confirmed it. I like to let the young people come to me. I feel a bit like a farmer who has sown abundantly and sees seedlings sprouting from the ground.

To avoid getting stuck or losing contact I always look for the combination of exit and voice that I discussed in "A Magical Divide." This makes me freer and does the same for you. At the same time, such an advanced recovery mechanism allows me to maintain a high level of efficiency. I have dedicated this piece to Daniela because she is a young woman from this year who is temporarily replacing Pasquale Napolitano in welcoming students to the department. Daniela is showing that she can do many things well at the same time and therefore *already* possesses recovery mechanisms that she needs to become more aware of. In a very endearing letter of reply she wrote to me: "What strikes me is the simplicity of your idea. It is as if, in that ambiguous drawing where you can see both an old woman and a beautiful woman, everyone saw only the old woman. Then someone (you) says: yes, the old woman is there. But you know, if you look carefully, you'll be able to see the beautiful woman as well. It's only a question of perspective!" Now the problem is not only seeing. One must also pursue the beautiful woman day after day. If some young people get to be good at this juggling exercise they will infect "everyone." I hope Daniela plays a role in this process.

When you work at my levels of intensity and endurance, you feel like you want to focus on regaining your strength. You have the pleasure of shopping and cooking (soberly) to promote recovery. Such things help you regain strength and even help you sleep. Many other activities become superfluous or irritating—a waste of time. I willingly go to the cinema only if I'm sure it will be worth it. And I'm not much interested in what the TV has to say—it's rare to find anything really useful. I need five minutes to unwind into an attitude of passivity that predisposes me to sleep—I suffer from insomnia. All in all, it is a somewhat monkish life, animated by great personal satisfaction.

"I wish I had 10 percent of your skills," exclaimed a friendly tall young man from Castellammare who had begun collecting signatures for the establishment of the National Evaluation Commission (Remember the first chapter of *Spender meglio*?). I think he's wrong, but that he raised a real problem—no one or hardly anyone can find the courage to compare themselves to me. Everyone or nearly everyone thinks of me as some kind of phenomenon. At my tender age, it really seems too much to come across as this "Rambo" who shows up out of the blue and puts everything in order!

Truth be told, I do not see myself as an extraordinarily gifted person. If anything, I am a Positano street kid who has always loved freedom above all else, who has acted according to conscience (perhaps mistakenly), and who got a good dose of stubbornness from Mother Nature. And in alternating phases I have built my life so that it has some actual utility. It's a long story. Maybe, if you really want to, we can start it by the fireplace some winter's night.

The outcome, though, I can tell you straightaway. Of course I have more experience, but I don't have that much strength. It is not true that we cannot compare ourselves—I try to put myself in your shoes all the time. The truth is that you do the opposite only rarely because you give in to laziness—you live utilizing a small amount of your energy and are only able to mobilize it in exceptional cases. So I become an extraterrestrial and the game is over. It is a game that does you no credit and above all does you no good. At the exams, a girl from Cisciano confessed that she had been silent for months because she was in awe of me. This came out in a burst of vitality, following my explicit provocation. In that moment I understood it all. It is essential that you interact with me the way I interact with you. It is essential that you stop thinking of me as a monster, a Rambo, a *deus ex machina* or an extraterrestrial and instead begin to confront me, perhaps in small steps, so that you can learn more while at the same time strengthening your own independent seat of judgment. Daniela continues, writing, "The extraordinary thing is that despite your leadership, you do not dominate us; you just show us the way. We're the ones who decide whether, how, and when to go our own way." This is what I conscientiously try to do. But you have to make the effort to see my world (as well as your own) precisely so that you can make better progress in yours. Basically, apart from the differences in age and experience, I just live a more focused and determined life than you do. In time you will discover that there are more focused and determined lives than mine. José Serra the Brazilian minister of economy who is of Calabrian descent is a case in point.

However, I can assure you, when you abandon laziness and by successive efforts push yourself toward the full use of your resources and capabilities (remember "My idea about slack"?) something will begin to stick with you. First, you will begin to live your life with a greater measure of autonomy. You will realize that it is foolish to fret, to get angry, or delude yourself. When you succeed you experience a kind of ironic split. Is it possible that I did it myself with the little strength I have? You will understand that if you still want to improve you have to give yourself more breathing room and at the same time more clarity and better timing—sometimes just a few words are enough, if they are well said. I am convinced that these are things you already have in your hands and that you glimpse them in flashes but fail to pursue them consistently. If not, why would you be so impressed by Eugenio Colorni—my students' "most beloved Italian"? Why else would you congratulate yourself when your exam goes well, or when you manage to write a super-thesis "piece"? Evidently you have discovered that you can do more than you thought you could do. I am reminded of a remark by Mita—the latest, very young super-thesis writer—who said she was amazed that she had been able to write the first part of her thesis on "Reinventing Government."

Even breathing space, clarity, and timing—is in reality within your reach. Theoretically, you can find it in the transition from tight to lose constraints and then to voice and exit. In practice it means learning to extricate yourself from psychological bondage and debt (personal, and to family and friends) as well as from lower priority tasks, so as to be "tuned in" and in full efficiency mode at the right time. You have to learn, folks; you have to learn to be simultaneously free and efficient, together with people you really like. This is where I come to the point.

When someone goes very far in using their abilities and resources, it should not be assumed that others will get the hint. Everyone will believe that only you can solve the problems that continually arise, and this external pressure will continually drive you to overdo it. But then it becomes clear that if things go on like this your own work will deteriorate. What is missing is breathing space, clarity, and timing, and to get these requires rowing in reverse.

Perhaps this was why I decided at a certain point to give everything. Of course, you always hope under the pressure of events to scrape together energy, freshness and money from somewhere. Then the realization dawns that no matter how hard you try, the vampire's thirst that assails you will not be quenched. So if you are really committed to what you are doing, my advice to yourself and others is to "give it everything." For some time, as you know, I have been doing the work of four people. And for some time, there has been a Nicoletta and Luca foundation (in a manner of speaking) that provides various Italian and foreign facilities. But only now have we scraped the bottom of the barrel; for example, by making a large part of the research fund available as secretarial and expense reimbursement—a little trick of encouragement that I think is producing good results.

At the psychological level this has two important consequences that everyone should know about. The first is that when you've really given everything there's nothing left in the tank (except your own self-destruction). This puts you at peace with your conscience. It is perfectly valid to think that you cannot do more than this in terms of quality, quantity and determination. If the desired results are not achieved it is not my fault—it is because of the objective situation, which always has to be faced with vigilant realism, taking the behavior of others into account. If, despite the difficulties, the situation is not bad, which is how it looks to me today (if we are able to put it to good use in Italy and the world) then the constraint accepted for oneself becomes a call for change in the behavior of others.

That was what I wanted to tell you. I ask for your intelligent and active help so that the truly extraordinary and exciting thing that we have been able to build together does not dissipate—which has unfortunately happened at other times in my life. I hope you are able to respond appropriately. I appeal to young people so that they can re-educate everyone with their insightful actions.

And so, after two feverish and intense days spent in Naples giving examinations to fifty young people and talking to many of you, and after a recovery day spent in bed writing this, I am at last drained and serene.

I send you my warmest regards,

Luca

Stefania Squillante

The Passions and the Interests[23]

Deceiving dichotomies

A few years ago, Luca argued the inconsistency of the contrast between passion (in the sense of love) and interest (in the sense of utilitarianism, personal advantage) with the following marriage metaphor:

No marriage can be based solely on interest or solely on passion. Sooner or later a man who marries a woman he is deeply in love with will want to know how much she earns or how much she is costing him, while someone pushed into marriage for base economic reasons will in time grow to appreciate his partner and learn to love her.

This example illustrates a point I think we can all agree on: the dichotomies invented by Western thought are nothing more than miserable attempts to harness reality within defined logical categories. Reality always leaps out in spades, and it appears to be most aptly described by the popular adage: the extremes meet.

As uplifting and above all liberating as the objection against a certain dogmatic and deceitful style of reasoning appears to be (and essentially is), we are all unfortunately still too attached to dichotomies, often pitting feelings against interests, and in our relational spheres, we ask questions along these lines: "How much does this or that person care about me and how much or for what purpose does he or she use me?" Or: "Why is everyone so self-interested (so that they don't feel love)?" Better yet: "Why doesn't anyone love me without demanding anything from me?"

---

[23] From *Italia vulcanica* n. 1 (2018): 82-84.

Sometimes it seems that everyone, sooner or later, wants something from us, and this observation can push me to the very sad conclusion that, therefore, no one loves me.

Which takes us right back to the logic of the dichotomy mentioned above.

This reminds me of a wonderful book by Maslow (1962), the one about the scale of needs, *Towards a Psychology of Being*. The text distinguishes between B type love (of being) and D type love (deficiency).

The first is completely disinterested, causing you to acquire the beloved object regardless of any relation of it to the whole. It is the rarest, the noblest—the true love of the other motivated solely by what the other is intrinsically.

The second kind of love arises to supply something we lack, something we need, even to fulfill a legitimate need such as the simple need to be loved. According to Maslow, and it is perfectly clear why, we all would like to be loved with a type B love but end up loving with a type D love, the one that sooner or later makes some kind of claim.

Luca and us

The relationship Luca forges with each of us, his kids, is not completely identified with either of these two types. Even this taxonomy turns out not to be infallible.

Refraining from classifying this bond, I will simply describe it. We can distinguish some of the steps toward the path of awareness, with the usual benefit of the inventory we assign to sequences (reversible, inverted, parallel rather than consecutive).

An initial realization

You discover that Luca loves you. When you sense this, you may believe that he will love you in any case, no matter what you do. After all, we all feel a little bit like his children, and from our experience as children we are used to thinking that a parent will eventually forgive your shortcomings and take you back in, wherever you are coming from.

But this is not exactly the way it is with Luca—indeed, it's not like this at all. If your behavior is out of line, ambiguous, or disengaged, he will first warn you, then reprimand you, and finally if your misconduct persists, he will show you the door.

That is when you understand that Luca is neither your father nor your mother.

The misunderstanding

Victims of our perverse Western nature, we are led to believe that if something has been proven false, then its opposite will certainly be true.

Going back to the dichotomy under discussion, we think: "If he wants something from us, then he doesn't love us." And this is followed almost immediately by the doubt: "But if he doesn't love us, what does he want from us?"

And here, since, as Socrates said, doubt is the father of knowledge, we are ready for a third step.

The inquiry

One may be left for a while wondering, "What does he want?"

The length of this phase and especially the content of the answers to this question are a function of the degree of cynicism we suffer from. But after some analysis, one cannot help but think again.

The discovery

Luca is emotionally interested in us, in each of us—in our lives, in our aspirations, in our potentials, in our needs. Generally, then, he offers you a second chance.

In short, he loves you, but that does not authorize you to

be a smartass or a free rider.

The trap

Finally, we have to overcome a last trap that Western thinking has set for us—the temptation to summarize at all costs.

Parallel tracks are not a kind of compromise of the type:

– I love you but I need you. Type D love

or

– I need you but I also love you. A disgusting mixture of utilitarianism and paternalism.

The surprise

Parallel tracks are on the contrary a surprising discovery.

Surprising ought to be the possibilist's favorite word.

True, Luca wants something from us, but what we think we are doing for him—victims as we are of an optical illusion—we are actually doing for ourselves, and the benefit is mostly ours.

(Are we perhaps too weak or scared to think that we are doing this for ourselves from the beginning?)

In this very strange relationship, the more you commit yourself to the common cause (possibilism, association, research, etc.), the more you gain for yourself, the less you feel used, and the more you feel gratified, wanted, loved.

You are useful but you are not being used and you are much more useful to yourself, however much effort you put in for others.

It doesn't often happen that what you do for someone is repaid—in fact, almost all religions try to convince us that our reward is somewhere else and that because of this they console us when we feel slighted.

This commitment Luca asks for, on the other hand, is immediately compensated, and in valuable currency—self-esteem, self-awareness, and intellectual, cultural, spiritual, and human growth. In other words, empowerment.

Maybe Luca doesn't know it, but he is applying the celestial rule of the Dao:

"Nurture all creatures but do not make them dependent." And like the Dao, "He acts but does not appropriate anything; he does not dwell on the results of his work and that is why they endure."

A delicate balance between doing too much and doing too little.

February 1994

Luca Meldolesi

Environment and Psyche[24]

Introductory report to the extended "experimental promotion group" meeting held in Monte Sant'Angelo on March 18, 1994 (revised notes).

Our experiment, which has now been going on for years, has gone through various phases—opening economics to other disciplines, theorizing, practical application to the Southern reality. In recent years it has seen significant acceleration thanks to better mastery of the subject and the greater presence we have been able to establish, both locally and in international relations. Yet this vigorous development, which has brought so many of us so much satisfaction, is now faced with difficulties that cannot easily be removed. These I would group under two headings. The first concerns understanding our responsibilities to the local environment, and the second the psychological aspects of our experience.

A difficult environment and a high moral profile
In the first place, in order to build our operation in a difficult environment like Naples, it is essential to maintain a high moral profile. Anyone who takes part, without exception, must be required to give up the pathological daily game which purports to get someone more than they deserve. As one of you said, nothing should be given away. Not only that, at the moment of breaking away from the familiar pattern one has to be prepared to pay the price of our criticism (implicit or ex-

---

[24] From *Italia Vulcanica* n. 1 (2018): 49-53.

plicit)—that is, to accept temporarily getting less than one deserves. Paradoxically, I have the idea that this is an important key to personal success, in that the advice it offers, conditions being what they are, is to invest in yourself, to elevate your own excellence and ultimately achieve much better results than you otherwise would have.

It so happens, just as in other markets, that those who hold a really strong position sooner or later do indeed break through.

Merit and exit/voice

This lesson, I think, based on the personal experience of some of us, contains a general meaning that applies to different aspects of our venture: to courses, exams, and all possible types of theses, as well as for the stages of the career that follows. The "maladie d'amour" so frequently diagnosed is so pervasive that we find it at every step, and at every step we must be able (with awareness and therefore purpose) to stand up to it. This is not easy. I think it is a real miracle that for years we have been able to present different courses, different exams, different theses, different postgraduate experiences through an original overall coherence which, as far as I know, is unparalleled. But I also think that to be able to progress further, we need to understand things better.

Despite the traditional tolerance of the Neapolitan setting, in emphasizing merit and commitment from a free and open perspective like the (Hirschmanian-Colornian-Falconian) positions we have identified has ended up provoking a contrary reaction. Overcrowded courses are disliked by colleagues and custodians, theses of too high quality (like Moody's AAAs) cause envy and annoyance, and also my publications abroad and the arrival of foreign professors who are too prominent and authoritative will probably end up ruffling feathers. In short, I sensed alarm bells—in a way I am returning to being

Mr. Too Much (too active, too productive, too popular, etc.), which is what happened to me in Rome in the 1970s.

On the other hand, if you look deeper, you unfortunately see that the issue is not only about teachers. Liliana's course and mine are to some extent preparatory in that they push students in the desired direction. But it is not easy to fight ambiguities nested in consciences. The memory of the courses will remain indelible—I often receive expressions of gratitude years later. Yet very few decide in the end to follow the path of merit and commitment. Behind the thousands of justifications given there is simply the personal difficulty of "getting along."

On that note, I would like to get rid of one of the many labels that have been attached to me. It is said that I am interested only in quality theses but come up short in the institutional task of training intermediate level graduates. This is a baseless claim that shows indirectly the way things stand. In fact, not only is it true that I have trained excellent "middle managers" such as Chiarello, Flagiello, Iannuzzo and Thomas; but I have also tried to do "the impossible" for young Neapolitan undergraduates. I accepted any type of thesis that was submitted. I have had all kinds of people graduate, even those who for a wide variety of reasons (of culture, health, family) struggled to get to the bare minimum. For the sake of decency (or if you like, moral rigor) I subjected myself to all kinds of corvée, including meeting with parents (not to mention grandparents!). Nicoletta accompanied me free of charge whenever we deemed it necessary. To explain the logic of my behavior I wrote "How to draw boundaries"[25]—a paper that I would like you to keep in mind. Finally, I posted on the bulletin board a simple set of regulations on thesis preparation [26] that corresponds to these experiences. *Sic stantibus rebus,* am I wrong to think that the aforementioned rumors are simply absurd?

---

[25] In *Italia Vulcanica* n. 1 (2018): pp. 45-46.
[26] In *Italia Vulcanica* n. 1 (2018): 62.

But this is not the point. The point is that working towards excellence requires a great deal of commitment, an unremitting exercise of will, a lasting effort at self-improvement—whatever your starting point and regardless of whether your finishing point is excellent, good or just enough.

Everyone who comes to see me knows that I will insist on value and commitment. Not only that, but they also know that at graduation sessions I defend the point of view of merit (including others) and that for this very reason I cannot reward those who do not deserve it. It is for that reason alone that I do not have "waiting lists."

On the other hand, the problem has recently taken on another aspect. For many years Liliana (to whom all of us—I want to emphasize this—are bound by feelings of affection, esteem, and admiration for what she has managed to build) has freely shuttled back and forth between our endeavor and the surrounding environment, among other things performing very useful liaison work. Recently, with her work on the state and her involvement in small business surveys, she has developed a fresh kind of creativity and made an important contribution to the formation of our promotion group. But as if to show how difficult the road she has taken is, in various aspects of university life Liliana has maintained a more conciliatory attitude. One of the consequences is that some students, although perhaps enthusiastic about my course, decide to put themselves on Liliana's waiting list.

Where is this taking us—I asked myself?

As you know, we have put every bit of our energy into building our perspective. The dedication of all the members of the organizing committee and the others around them has been very high in recent months. We have built a useful home support base. To counter the backlash unintentionally triggered by our initiative, we tried to move astutely between exit and voice (e.g., by renouncing *pro bono pacis* a certain Departmental role and by self-restraining, as it were, our already fading "academic clout"). We have worked hard to combat isolation in different parts of the country and internationally. But there is always a shortage of money. In any case, greater awareness would not hurt.

A psychological service

Now to the second point. If this is the way things are, if in order to combat the current trend each of us has to fight a battle aimed at elevating our own worth in absolute and relative terms, then it becomes apparent that along with the intellectual work we need to perform a sustained labor of self-persuasion and psychological adjustment. I think this dimension ought to be given much greater weight than it has had up to now. It is something that is not easy to bring into focus and it has instead often been passed over, whether out of demureness or lack of knowledge. In reality, it is essential to unceasingly encourage each other and others as well to "look inwards" in a simple, good-natured and self-deprecating way, to cope with the individual change that is so essential to the growth of one's work.

This means, as my psychiatrist nephew explained to me, that along with "food for thought" we are actually providing a psychological service, a service that starts from the course and runs all the way up to our committee—I could cite dozens of episodes. And the beauty of it is that the basic exercise in all this "trafficking" in one way resembles and in another goes beyond the best psychological practices. The idea of changing one's perspective (in terms of mood, mind, and place) in order to see oneself in a different light is typical of therapy. And moreover, we take pleasure in relating this to specific intellectual knowledge that we master on merit and mix into different environments. For example—we have extended a certain sense of family to the committee and at the same time, through the foundation, we have extended a certain "committee sense" to our families.

This whole area midway between psychology and reflecting about our own practice is largely unexplored. We did it spontaneously, although it is of course influenced by Nicoletta's and my experience of the 1970s and our introspective work to overcome the resulting difficulties. The issue now—I think— is to understand it and make better use of it. And this means investing in those studies—of Simmel, Colorni, the history of psychology, learning theory and empowerment in its broadest sense—that can sustain our effort. We need to translate them into writings and parts of the course, make them familiar enough to turn everyone into "barefoot psychologists," to borrow a well-known Chinese expression. We are Colornian enough to know that if we can manage to really get inside the problem (perhaps through repeated campaigns) it will come naturally to us to apply the lesson to all our work. Here, then, is a "new frontier" that, once conquered, will enable us to break through the "bottleneck" restricting our initiative, so that it can be expanded to include many more people.

Luca Meldolesi

Five Liberations[27]

The present "psychology campaign" has for me been a source of numerous surprises.

1. First of all there is the Colornian aspect of it. The solution was just around the corner, but without the effort to find it, which involved breaking down personal resistance (dictated by the quiet life, implosions, inertia, lack of awareness, ignorance, laziness, impotence, risk-aversion, etc.) the road would never have opened. So here, too, intellectual boldness pays off and propels you higher. But it is not enough to identify the path. You have to walk it, otherwise you risk being re-absorbed.

2. Then there is the collective aspect. I felt like I was on my own in a knife fight against a recalcitrant environment. But it was a consequence of self-isolation. Now that the veil of Maya has been lifted, I realize that I am by no means alone—that all around me, and not that far away, other interesting initiatives are springing up, perhaps a little confused, but reasonably balanced and unburdened (at least in part) by traditional extremism.

3. Again, if you go down to the specific level, my way of teaching naturally fits into a larger pattern. It is part of a general alternative that claims to put down roots and establish itself in soil that is purely educational: individual learning and achievement. This aspect of the outcome is especially salient in our

---

[27] From *Italia Vulcanica*, n. 1 (2018): 54.

case—it can be said that by starting with economic policy we have interpreted the trend of change in a more rigorous and useful way.

4. Another aspect of convergence/difference is the increased "personal work." The release of internal psychological forces is geared toward individual and professional growth. This opens the vast field of experimentation typical of our experience, which I explained in "Environment and Psyche." It would be worthwhile to reconstruct together (through testimony and re-flection) how we were able to achieve certain results.

5. Finally, it seems to me, personally, that I have swept aside some defensive barriers that were admittedly useful in the past, but which were also a source of embarrassment—a way I have of "getting riled," of attacking the stupidity and impudence of others, of committing blunders of warning, perhaps to high-ranking professors. Such behavior stems from the intimate need not to be overpowered, but it might serve no purpose if the optics of the work became more explicit, accepted and mindfully experienced, further solidifying the astuteness of exit-voice.

22 March 1994

Luca Meldolesi

The Mentor[28]

I was reminded of a remark of Albert's when he was in Naples. After getting a good look at your faces, he told me in a whisper, "The job of 'mentor' is important." It was only later that I realized it was a promotion in the field.

What did Albert mean? It is useful to recall that in the United States he was known as "a good coach." Of course, adjustments of scale must be made. In any case, the compliment mentioned above comes from none other than the person capable of setting up Captain Cardoso's Big Brazil. In short, no great coach minds recognizing the work done by the trainer of a junior team....

The term 'mentor' is German, designating the initiator, the comrade in the lead. Albert's mentor was Henry Ehrmann, seven years his senior, who introduced him to Hegelian philosophy and social-democratic ideas. A few years ago, together with Albert, Ehrmann received an honorary degree from the Science Po in Paris. Unfortunately he died in December—I won't be able to interview him. I will have to make do with the letter that Albert wrote for his funeral and that Lisa read in San Diego on his behalf.

So to understand more about it, I can only question myself. How did I get to be a good 'mentor'? A thunderclap in the night reminded me of my harsh initiation, which along with a militant (and irreverent) attitude gave me the strength not to give up on myself, but to continually seek direction for myself and others—which instead shows how disoriented I often feel.

But doesn't this reassessment of a stern initiation represent

---

[28] From *Italia Vulcanica* n. 2 (2019): 39-41.

a reversal of judgment? Doesn't it run counter to what I have written elsewhere about economics? It does not.

Severe initiation is not necessarily related to intransigence, or to economics. It simply concerns a period in which, under the impetus of a specific project, the subject is able to "cultivate" his or her own hard and determined inner spirit, which will be on board for life. Harshness is thus related to the ability to make the most of one's own energy. My best thesis students know well that at a certain point I have been able to get them to cross this Rubicon and to "forge" them in such a way that they will then be able to utilize this "secret force" when the demands of their studies and life require them to do so. Being tough on yourself so as to then become active and open—this lesson of Colorni's is so agreeable to me that I tried to put it into practice more than two decades in advance of Albert's (2020) reporting of it.

It has come back to me how I got this way. In 1965-66 I had a weekly appointment with Joan Robinson. I had to bring her a four-page paper based on some of the literature (usually a book and four or five articles) on a topic that she assigned me. I was expected to master this literature and (if possible) have something to say about it. Come rain or shine, in sickness or health, no force in the world could have deterred me from my inner need to succeed with Joan.

Joan dressed in the Pakistani style, with a long white braid. She was the terror of lecturers because she would interrupt them, going to the blackboard and drawing pictures (like a spade, a factory or a school desk). Her intelligence was like lightning, as was the defiance she was not afraid to hurl at anyone she did not like.... including, of course, Robert Solow and Paul Samuelson.

Luca

Paolo Di Nola

Intimate Confessions of a Satisfied Supervisor[29]

This paper in part returns to a letter ("homo socialis animal") I wrote to Luca a few months ago.

The subject (for those who may not have read it), summed up in the ambitious title, was the inescapability of collaboration (of political commitment, if you like). Basically, I think that individual growth can't do without collaboration and communication—the happy[30] 'compromise' with others.

Obviously, there are other mechanisms that enable someone to follow the path of personal cultural enrichment—a lot depends on individual character!

Nevertheless, I am "obliged"(!) to say which of them I think is better based on the limited personal experience of these years. What follows are therefore reflections of a participant observer (as our sociologist would say)—that is, not theoretical postulates but direct experiences.

Perhaps you know that one (among others) of my small "obsessions" is nurturing interpersonal relationships—I assure you this is not just a quirk!

Obviously, I took (and continue to take) emblematic lessons in effectiveness from this exercise.

This way I have of looking at things brings together various themes that we have dealt with under different circumstances and for different reasons:

---

[29] From *Italia Vulcanica* n. 1 (2018): 100-105.
[30] I use the adjective "happy" in the sense of "desired" and "unforced."

- Collaboration in working groups;[31]
- Supervision;[32]
- Mentoring and individual psychological growth;[33]
- Support for the Mezzogiorno.[34]

These themes are not separated by watertight bulkheads. Thinking about one of them carries you logically to the others in a single logical progression.

Collaboration in working groups has yielded important results. there are personal cases of real enhancement of work capabilities that clearly came from the stimulus of group work.

Undoubtedly, collective thinking has a catalyzing function in individual creativity—some projects (theses, for example) often spring from the numerous insights gathered in discussions.

The way I see it, this is the normal utility of active participation in a working group.

The corollary (desired condition) of these observations (also quite obvious, if you like) is that there is also a "return" in terms of social utility. Sooner or later the group will be enriched in its turn by the contribution of the individual's intellectual creation—otherwise, the relationship becomes parasitic which, indeed, can easily happen!

This appeal does not advocate a principle or wish for the collectivization of intellectual property—everyone thinks and creates by and for themselves.

At the same time, by virtue of a *civil* quid pro quo relationship and a shared *intellectual* morality, behavior that is totally indifferent to the common interest is not acceptable.

---

[31] I refer to the organizational efforts made in carrying out the research on Act 44/1986, a law providing incentives to young Southern entrepreneurs.

[32] The issue is kept alive by everyone's ongoing needs and the activity of Luca, Liliana, and Nicoletta. But also, Gianni's, Ciro's, Valeria's, Leonardo's, Enzuccio's and to a limited degree, mine.

[33] In reference to the mentoring in Act 44/1986.

[34] I refer to Luca's speeches and writings on the subject.

Membership in our association must implicitly include this normal willingness to let everyone participate in the things you do or have done yourself.

I consider supervision to be a form of cooperation.

In this function, cultural forces of different origins and with different purposes are combined. In part, it is a form of "Beatricean" commitment to companionship in the "bright Elysian fields of Knowledge." In that sense, it is a form of mentoring.

Between supervisor and supervisee, a relationship should be created that takes on all the characteristics of Act 44-style mentoring. External assistance, that is—which, when necessary, can also include a great deal of participation—without risking replacing the beneficiary in his or her natural tasks.

Being able to modulate and control supervision is a difficult art when you are trying to drag along wagons that are broken or bogged down! Without intending to denigrate, this can be a common condition (with obvious personal distinctions) among those who have joined us recently (but not only—I am also thinking of so-called "veterans" in need of reeducation!) and who will engage in research or thesis work.

To quote myself, in these cases the "headway"[35] doesn't come right away and additional patience and effort are required. In these circumstances the danger is that a dependency will be created—*development* occurs, but *without autonomy*[36] and without responsibility.

Supervision is a complex function which, as part of a collaborative relationship between supervisee and supervisor, implements a pedagogical process.

---

[35] I am quoting the paradigm of "towing with headway," Paolo di Nola, Gragnano, 1994.

[36] It is perhaps superfluous to note that the expression is taken from the title of the book by C. Trigilia (1994).

The supervisor should possess a "cultural differential that must be effectively transferred"[37] to the supervisee.

This cultural differential has various origins:

– It exists previous to the supervision (so there is a relative presumption of recognizable supervisory ability in those with work experience);
– It is acquired during supervision for various reasons:

a) Because it is the supervisee who explicitly asks for advice on topics about which the supervisor does not know much (or, as happened to me, knows nothing);
b) Because it is the supervisor who independently discovers his or her own shortcomings and works hard to eliminate them;
c) Because, in an emblematic reversal of sequences, it is the supervisee who transfers certain knowledge to the supervisor, which the latter is able to rework, connect, and mix with other knowledge in his or her possession, creating a new way of interpreting and using the new or pre-existing knowledge.

In general, what emerges from situations a), b), and especially c) is the near coincidence of supervision and collaboration. Enrichment goes both ways, and the relationship strengthens the supervisee but also the supervisor.

Some of the important pedagogical functions of supervision may be summarized as follows:

1. Teach how to organize the job. This is the first thing a supervisor should push for. No idea can materialize without a work agenda (explicitly viewed as open to variation

---

[37] The expression comes from Claudia Corsi' thesis *L'assistenza alla creazione d'impresa: l'esperienza del tutoraggio nella legge 44/86 attraverso casi empirici*, Naples, 1994

during the course of the work, anticipating the possibility of following unexpected paths discovered along the way). It is important to ask the supervisee to construct it, but also that it be corrected and refined in group discussion.

The most important points in this guiding agenda are:

Identifying the specific area, sector and topic to be covered in a natural process of progressive "zooming in."

Indicating the points that the work should be based on while avoiding falling into a logic of prerequisites[38] (paradoxically, to speak with awareness about the problems of the Mezzogiorno it would be appropriate to delve into the causes that led to the fall of the Western Roman Empire and the descent of the Goths and Lombards into southern Italy. While this advice is rational on the level of historical perspective it is methodologically impractical).

Indicating the sources with this principle of concentration of focus in mind.

Setting time deadlines. These serve to keep work tension high (while avoiding the creation of states of anxiety or depression) and to provide for flexibility.

Program opportune moments for summarizing and thinking about what has been done not least for the purpose of adjusting the sights for the next stage.

2. Encourage the correct wording of questions. "Knowing how to ask" is a fundamental tool for supervisory success. The temptation to satisfy badly formulated questions or requests[39] should be resisted. It is important to make clear

---

[38] This is similar to the defect of development project planners discussed by A.O. Hirschman (1958) in *The Strategy of Economic Development*.

[39] "I would like to know what topic to do my thesis on ... And how long will it take me—two months or two years?" are typical badly formulated questions. At best, the supervisor can help the supervisee "figure out" what topic corresponds to their true interests. Giving an immediate answer to the first question is taking over an exclusive function of the supervisee. On the question of "how long," I never know what to say because the answer requires esoteric powers of foreknowledge that are not obligatory.

what the flaw in them is and to bring out—as spontaneously as possible—what is considered correct.

3. In general, help build a method of work that suits the individual's personality (pace of work, resistance to fatigue, inclination toward the theoretical or the practical, etc.), gradually moving the (qualitative) bar higher, but keeping in mind that at a certain point—especially in the case of theses—this rate of advance will not continue. A particular of the method concerns the connection between sources (libraries, journals, articles, etc.) and original creativity. Advising about how to utilize sources ("...should I summarize this page or can I copy it?") is a fundamental issue. What needs to be stimulated is the ability to connect, compare, and bring out similarities and differences among various readings on the same theme. Knowing how to make connections is already an important expression of creativity. The supervisor should know how to help bring to light underlying connections that have escaped the supervisee.

4. Ask for ways to escape from dead ends while rejecting claustrophobic behavior. A very common attitude is one in which the supervisee gets into trouble when faced with bottlenecks (initial, along the way, final) in the project, and instead of striving to overcome them by sheer simplicity, falls prey to a form of anxiety that paradoxically, gets him or her more and more tangled in the net. In such cases, overthought attempts at liberation should be blocked and a decision should be invited between two alternatives: either explicitly point out (in the text of the thesis or paper) that the aspect in question will remain unaddressed in order to get on with the original work program or go deeper and attempt to clarify it and abandon the original program. Usually, doing both of these (completing the original path and also tackling a new and unforeseen theme), within the same project, is not advisable. The supervisor should be able to weigh up the costs and benefits of the

two options, keeping in mind that in general, it is not necessarily the case that the second one (changing course to swim into a current that at the moment is more stimulating) is best if it requires sacrificing the remainder of a project that had seemed to promise equally interesting results.

In my experience, I think I have succeeded to some extent in putting these approaches into practice.

One important aspect (to think about *ex post*) is understanding what the goal of supervision is. Identifying the purposes of supervision serves as a "caveat" for the supervisor's own expectations, thus heading off any disappointment with the results.

In my view, the success of supervision is measurable not only by the successful achievement of productive autonomy and high product quality or the training of a promising sector expert, researcher, educator, or scholar (goals that I consider, however, the main "reason why" of supervision). One other significant result is also to help people discover their own shortcomings and aptitudes.

Guiding the supervisee in an in-depth analysis of his or her own work can help uncover illusion and lead to the discovery of new interests.

Supervision (or more precisely, supervised work) can thus take on the function of a tool for the further psychological growth of the person supervised.

It is in fact possible that experiencing an intellectual adventure will bring out interests in entirely different things previously overlooked or ignored: oneself, work, family, the study of mollusks, Chinese cooking, love for the castles of the Loire, etc.

In the spirit of our association the supervisor is thus an agent of natural selection.

It goes without saying that certain personal interests (fully respectable, not to censured or oppressed) are unrelated to the Association's typical activities.

Therefore, the discovery of "third-party" interests always involves a re-verification of the willingness (and mutual benefit) of continuing to belong to a group that aims at very specific cultural ends (and always keeping in mind the potential—almost always possible—compatibility of such personal interests with those ends).

Luca, Liliana and Nicoletta have raised some foals that have turned into thoroughbred horses (Gianni, Ciro, Laura, Tito, Maurizio, Walter, Valeria and the very promising Enzuccio), and the association needs to collaborate and continue this activity.

The necessary tools are already available:

- Supervision: considered not as an activity of control but an activity of external support providing stimulation to know and improve oneself. In this way, our association also becomes a point of reference for "weak subjects,"— for those (first and foremost: me) who need guidance to embark on autonomous cultural development.
- Natural selection—spontaneous, but also induced by supervision. This tool should be used to avoid indiscriminate overcrowding with regard to access or permanence in the association when its purposes are in conflict with the real interests of the associated member. It is a "border control" to protect the quality level of the group.

In short, collaboration, supervision/tutoring, and awareness of one's tasks (and interests) are the tools for inducing bottom-up, accountable, inclusive, meritocratic, and selective development that applies to all Mezzogiornos: the one in Italy is the one in each of us.

I thank Liliana Bàculo, who encouraged me to think and write about these things.

Gragnano, 28 October 1994

Vincenzo Marino

Subversion and Self-subversion[40]

Reading Albert Hirschman[41] along with the experience of planning and launching our Association, I have been inspired to put together some observations on the themes of subversion and self-subversion, and policy and psychology.

In *Spender meglio è possibile* Luca applied a method I would call researching (and applying) the psychological effects of policy (and economic policy) choices. Throughout the book, as background, the importance of evaluation is highlighted—assessing policies in relation to the effects (all the effects) they produce.

This issue is particularly important in our Southern context—a backward society, slow and almost impervious to change (or where change is constantly undervalued and denied) produces young people who are vibrant but sometimes oppressed by familial and intellectual provincialism. Faced with this, anyone who wants to challenge this state of affairs has to address the problem of what policies to use. Now fighting underdevelopment requires combating daily habits, generalized apathy, the encumbrance of underdevelopment, and an intellectual environment that leaves things as they are while suppressing positive initiative and the desire for change. I'm thinking, in other words, of the idea of "cognitive dissonance."

To paraphrase Albert, "the art of promoting development perhaps consists, first and foremost, of multiplying opportunities to stumble upon dissonance-inducing actions and instilling

---

[40] From *Italia Vulcanica* n. 1 (2018): 87-90.
[41] I refer to the book-interview *Crossing Boundaries* (Hirschman, 1998) and to the typescript in preparation for the 6 November 1994 conference, which Luca has graciously provided.

a principle of commitment to it", through various kinds of stimuli, such as projects that are engaging and inclusive, and using means, for example, like towing with headway.

Breaking away from bad habits, proposing a new way of doing things, stimulating others to adopt it—but then letting them learn to act on their own, free and independent.

This way of understanding the politics of change, focusing attention on the psychological aspects of change, seems to me "subversive" and revolutionary because it subverts mindsets—entrenched and "fossilized" ways of thinking—and because it subverts the tendency to disillusionment and disappointment—"fracasomania."

This idea of subverting minds lies, I believe, at the heart of Luca's special interest in all of us. I believe that we represent, individually and collectively, a development project in which each of us is investing something in terms of intellectual effort, commitment, desire to stand out, participatory passion, professional training, skills, friendship etc.

On close inspection, our Association project responds to each of the stages mentioned above.

In a first, fairly long phase, the idea "came down" from above. Repeatedly and on various occasions Luca tried to depict the idea of a stable and autonomous structure, of something that was created and directed by and addressed to young people—and that he was no longer the only one pulling the wagon of intellectual education. This phase of proposing and towing is definitely a "subversive activity of subversive policy." The feeling of being charged with responsibility and ambition has certainly stirred the waters, stimulating us to take action and be productive.

Now, we have taken possession of "our" Association project—we are creating it "with Luca" and no longer "because it's what Luca wants"! I remember some of the phrases most often repeated in one of the first students-only meetings in Caserta: "... but I don't quite understand what the professor wants..."; "... I believe that this is what the professor would like us to do..." and so on. Today, in the place of such phrases it is more common to hear others, of a different tone: "...what would you expect from the Association..."; "...I believe that we have a lot of work to do at the level of communication..." etc.

We are surely more in control of the situation and, it seems to me, we want to be. In other words, we have entered the "headway" phase.

Some chain reactions and self-subversions

In my opinion, what I have called "subversive policy" ends up generating real chain reactions—the feeling of being part of something important and exciting fuels the export of enthusiasm even into lateral fields such as thesis preparation. At least this is my own experience.

My sense is that the presence of an associated activity linked to that of being a student and writing a thesis promotes a breaching of the watertight compartments we are accustomed to living with (8 hours of study, 1 hour playing soccer, the weekend of recreation, etc.) and promoting the development of our very existence in an "interdisciplinary" direction. The aspect of life that involves the Association, the university and doing research is pushing harder and harder to achieve the same rights of citizenship in our daily round as recreation, affection, and family; perhaps precisely because it is recreation, affection, and friendship that the rest of life rests on.

Another aspect, intimately related to the "subversive policies of the mind," is learning self-subversion. Within this mechanism of towing with headway[42] we feel stimulated to explore our doubts further and critically reexamine what we

---

[42] Cf. P. Di Nola, *Intimate Confessions of a Satisfied Supervisor* above.

thought were long-held certainties. A capacity for self-subversion, as systematic and natural, so to speak, as the capacity in each of us to challenge ourselves and ask questions, is coupled with an "induced self-subversion"—induced by towing with headway. This is a self-critical capacity stimulated by a subversive policy that works within us to foster processes of learning and change. I have the impression that this "induced self-subversion," as I have called it, is the real disruptive element in our psychological and behavioral structures. Policy should stimulate changes, but it cannot fully engineer them. Hirschman argued that if one day we were to witness the total success of the social sciences (and therefore also of social policy) we should be prepared to witness the failure of the human being.

And therefore, even "subversive policy" needs to have allies in order to succeed. It needs a Trojan horse to smooth the way—it needs to spark a desire for self-subversion that leads individuals themselves to seek the road to change, to grow, to develop.

After an initial phase of towing, or at any rate along with the towing, it is we who have to have the will to change, to grow, to improve; it is only our own will to "extricate ourselves," our cooperation and our participation that can transform us from more or less heavy trailers into powerful tractors capable of towing other people.

I firmly believe that the existence of a stable structure, such as the Association, which aims at improving the quality of research (and more ambitiously of life) should serve precisely as a driving mechanism for towing with headway.

In this sense, the management team appointed by the Assembly will have to take responsibility for policy and strategy choices, the most appropriate methodologies for constantly improving the quality of individual and group research, the behavior of individual members, and the external "value" of research products.

The "Directorate" should study what tools to use (along with supervision and evaluation) to stimulate self-subversion, unleash positive energy and suppress uncooperative attitudes. Here, I have to say, Paolo's letter is illuminating—it is the true point of departure, the true frame of reference for the behavior of future "instructors." I would like to publicly thank Paolo for having cleared up many things that had up to now only been hinted at!

I believe that the events of the last few weeks, the interviews with members, their analysis and evaluation, the first meetings with Leonardo Ditta and Liliana Bàculo for the establishment of the Latin America Group, the days of group work, the collaboration with "the omnipotent" Nicola, and some moments of reflection with Maurizio, Valeria, and Walter have revealed remarkable human and intellectual capacities, a truly exhilarating friendly and "familial" atmosphere, and a desire (which has gradually turned into knowledge) to build "something wonderful" together!

I have great confidence in our ability to rise to the task.

24 October 1994

Vincenzo Marino

On Who We Are and Where We Come From. And on Where We're Going[43]

"For a tear is an intellectual thing", William Blake

When Luca informed me that the book on Colorni would be called "The Courage of Innocence," (Colorni, 1998) I was struck by a thrill of sincere emotion that transported me back in time.

In my high school days, I was among the leaders of the Neapolitan student movement, excited about my activism and the role of the politically engaged young man that was increasingly being attached to me.

We took in the explosion of the nuclear reactor at Chernobyl with grave and profound concern: after major debates, political meetings, and discussions with the professor of mathematics and physics, we decided that the 9th Scientific High School "Piero Calamandrei" would become the first denuclearized school in Italy. At the time this choice had only symbolic value, but in light of the subsequent referendum it would also have profound political value, and it filled us with joy.

Despite his past as a militant and as a Communist leader, my father was puzzled by all this "wasted energy," and to tell the truth, the constant strikes, occupations, and "denuclearizations" were so frequent that little time was left for the rest. And the "rest" consisted of love, soccer and, finally, books. Nevertheless, I was among the best in my class, which was among the best in the school.

Concerned about my exuberance, my father turned to the

---

[43] From *Italia Vulcanica* n. 1 (2018): 91-93.

professors who, not so paradoxically, turned out to be more activist and politically engaged than their students.

Filomena Capalbo was the history and philosophy teacher. Despite her diminutive figure, she was a remarkable character of great cultural and political depth. My father expressed to her his concern about a son who was so easily stirred up, so dedicated to political commitment, so exuberant and yet "so impractical that his books place last in his daily commitments."

The answer the teacher gave my father is at the root of the emotional thrill I have held inside for so long, and that Luca, with his disclosure of a few days ago abruptly revived: "Mr. Marino, you cannot even imagine how difficult it is becoming nowadays to find young people who can laugh and cry sincerely, who are trustworthy and open to others, and who have the courage to be innocent."

This anecdote would remain only a cherished personal memory if it were not of use to me in clarifying some issues concerning the life of our Association, the ways we all should behave within it, our very way of being.

The most important problem that the office of the presidency has faced in recent days is how to stimulate collaboration and cooperation within the Association and, conversely, how to combat free riding, mistrust, and mutual intolerance.

Inevitably, individualism and free riding crop up whenever a sacrifice of private interests is imposed by interests that are collective and public. This happens, Catalano would say, when private and public interests are openly and objectively in conflict.

A second essential point (my thanks to Luca for "unveiling" it) is that it is especially difficult, if not counterproductive, to impose rules of behavior from above which would if tested prove to be sterile. In fact, apart from the authoritarian risks in such a strategy (which on this point would be in open conflict with the spirit of the Association itself), it often ends up setting rules whose value is merely formal and are not respected by anyone.

How then to solve the problem? How can we manage to avoid speculative and self-interested apathy, and the non-communication, wary and jealous rather than shy, of one's own experiences—obtaining free information, that is, without giving anything in return?

The solution is to nullify the public-interest / private-interest trade-off, to break down distrust by not being distrustful, to create democracy and respect by being democratic and respecting others, and to get information by giving it unselfishly!

It is fighting the downward spirals of a life made up only of private interests (too often even "in official acts!").

Paraphrasing Luca, having the courage of innocence—the courage of free and benevolent openness, and of love and friendship.

On closer inspection, this phrase is actually our battle cry; it is our manifesto, it is us in our innermost depths. It is the innocence that sets us apart from others, that gives us the strength to experiment in our own small way with the method of democracy and openness, that distinguishes us from an environment (including academic) that appears to us permeated with pettiness and small mindedness. The good fortune of having Luca and Nicoletta should convey to everyone that what we are learning from them is not simply a research methodology and a passion for what is possible (important things in themselves) but essentially a modus vivendi, a philosophy of life and relationships based precisely, and consciously, on their own friendly openness to all of us.

Those who want to be with us must therefore learn this spirit, identify with it. This is because that phrase, which many years ago the professor said to my father, has stuck to my soul, and I have the conceit that it is the true discriminator on which membership in the Association is based.

P.S. I thank Luca Meldolesi for soliciting these reflections in a letter addressed to me. I also thank him for the choice of the title of the book.

Torre Annunziata, 15 December 1994

Luca Meldolesi

Spontaneity and Energy[44]

Yesterday, December 27, the whimsical Potentino (Gianni Molinari) was present in spirit. A few days earlier he had sent an email about organization. As soon as I saw it, I thought "not again!" But he was right. Coincidentally I was working on Colorni's article on "spontaneity as a form of organization" (Colorni 2019, p. 25-32) and had just shown Nicoletta a beautiful passage. She asked me for it to respond to Gianni. The email reached Maurizio Maturo, who immediately attached it to the wall of his election committee. In a flash, aided by the email, we had made a sudden leap forward.

For younger people this reasoning requires an explanation. For so many years, glory days included, my generation was burdened by the organizational problem—Leninists or Luxemburgers? Should spontaneity be organized or not? Now with Eugenio's (and Albert's) reasoning the whole aspect of the issue has changed. The question is not whether spontaneity is a force for change. Obviously it is—Eugenio's, that is, Rosa Luxemburg's and yours (not, as Colorni points out, the one Lenin talks about). The problem is to strengthen, energize, and develop that spontaneity as a form of organization. (For the sake of accuracy, I would like to add that here, too, the book was the go-between because to close Colorni's anthology I had brought to Naples Ciro Coppa's excellent thesis, still awaiting publication. His timely reading suggested that I sort my ideas as follows).

But what does it mean in concrete terms, you will be won-

---

[44] From *Italia Vulcanica* n. 9 (2020): 64-68.

dering? To more fully grasp this it is best to use Albert's language and to define Eugenio's political spontaneity as energy deployed for the purpose of change. It is not potential energy, and it is not energy directed toward other ends (corporate, clientelist, mystical or otherwise). When I spoke on this point yesterday, I said that it is essential for us to unleash our internal energy. For the organization to grow hand in hand with intellectual processing we must develop appropriate inductive mechanisms that enable the full mobilization of internal energy. We have unearthed some— Colornially, others may be just around the corner.

We can view our educational experience (one of the best in the country) as a multi-stage rocket. It started with courses as incubation periods: the student perhaps comes to tick off an exam and then instead has to sweat it out. To produce this liberating effect, Liliana, Nicoletta and I use attractive and instructive materials. In addition, I have long made use of insurmountable constraints—such as attendance, separation into letters, the two exam schedules—to increase the drive to release energy and so to avoid the traditional exam. Indeed, instead of a cost, the exam becomes highly beneficial because it forces the student to actually learn something. Now the attendance requirement has been abandoned (because of the large number of students, because of the routinization of the course), but I have not abandoned the attempt to talk to everyone who wants to talk to me, and I prefer to drag out exams for months on end rather than water down this decisive tool. Each year, in short, the courses, their spontaneity deliberately enhanced through a direct psychological relationship with the students, yield a prodigious outpouring of energy, part of which is then channeled into theses.

Even in this second stage, things have now settled down. Students have to do a thesis—we push them toward a thesis of personal satisfaction and collective interest. Together, these two aspects powerfully stimulate their latent energies. Of course, the story of every thesis, even those that are most successful, is peppered with setbacks, attempts at circumvention, illusions, and so on. But if the teacher actually performs his or her function of unlocking energy, students will end up giving what they are capable of giving. This is the problem of the super-thesis, which nowadays stands alongside that of the normal thesis and the short thesis. The creation of thesis groups has proven essential in bringing students out of isolation, allowing them to learn from each other and from older students and graduate students. The question of quality remains the central issue, along with the question of the full utilization of products (the publication of articles and thesis excerpts for "The Poplar," the general reworking of results).

But then comes the difficult aspect of our organization. While it is possible to say that the first two stages are relatively settled, this is not yet the case for the stages that follow: involving on-campus graduates, students in postgraduate courses, clerical staff, external employees, managers. Each of these categories has its own specific needs and must be monitored with appropriate elements of inducement to head off wastage and free up energy. Here our steps are still uncertain, but there are many interesting insights, and the current organizational question is riding on them.

In brief. I really liked when Liliana referred to the graduates on campus and explained that the *argent de poche* that we now try to provide them with serves to hush up the parents and provide some peace of mind during what is essentially a training period. I would add that along with its direct effect *argent de poche* must have an indirect one—removal of a justification for the tendency to under-perform (and the so-called post-graduation crisis).

Moreover, it should not be seen as welfare (i.e., it must be given in exchange for work) even if we do have to worry about those who are without money. In essence it functions here as a supplementary mechanism to those of individual training and collective interest. This has also been true for some theses such as those of Angela and Maria Brigida. Thus, meeting the short-term need for a few hundred thousand liras is transformed into a major boost in the mobilization of personal energy.

On the other three roles our ideas are still rough. But it is worth jotting something down.

a) Graduates who study in Italy and abroad. Generally, their courses are very taxing. We must meet them halfway by not exacerbating their "cross pressures." At the same time, it is important to avoid losing contact and to ask them for a few little jobs that are not burdensome.

b) The experience of employed graduates like Gianni, Laura, Stefania, and Ciro us that it is essential for us to harness their positive energies. But this requires a fusion of professional interest and public interest that takes their current condition into account. Therefore, it is also a matter of independent spheres and networking. Dealing with this peculiarity requires experience and, above all, building a network they can be positioned in.

c) External graduates are all those who come into contact with us at their request or ours (alumni, former *compagnons d'armes*, newcomers, etc.). Here we are squarely within the web that we need to build in the half-full/half-empty relationship with the government.

And finally, managers—a key issue. The leadership role should be divided and delegated as much as possible—we need to create dozens, hundreds of leaders in our organization and network. Every material and moral inductive effort toward this end, it seems to me, is justified. But we should have no illusions: the problem will continue to plague us. Here it seems to me that the steps forward are 1) explicit recognition of the general need, 2) acceptance of the actual role: Vincenzo first, Maurizio now, 3) the idea of some kind of rotation, 4) interest in specific areas, and 5) an understanding of the upheaval involved and of the breakthrough it represents.

What I would like to see added to all this is a keen perception of the issue of mobilizing individual energies as a specific and general problem to be tackled in an atmosphere of creativity, fond emulation and the most absolute freedom. Herein lies a decisive key to our itinerary. "What do you think Nicola?" "That will become clear in my work." I am very happy with this answer.

PART III

Education, Research, and Change

Luca Meldolesi

Recovering from the Camorra[1]

[...] My starting point is one of the most abnormal phenomena that exist in Europe today—the expansion of the Italian criminal economy and the vast nebula of complicity that surrounds it. Personally, my purpose was twofold: to look a slice of that reality in the face and to open the way for an observation of the Southern condition that is (paradoxically) out of the ordinary. But I must confess that these aims did not travel on their own—the inquiry into the Neapolitan Camorra that follows also arose from the need to find the signs, dialectics, and methodologies of a possible change.

A FACT-FINDING INQUIRY

For a considerable time, the Camorra has been deeply corroding the social structure of some neighborhoods in Naples and entire areas of Campania. In recent years this permanent epidemic seems to have entered a phase of resurgence. Every so often the light of public attention is directed at it—local, national, or European. But then the phenomenon slips back into the shadows and continues to spread, expanding the range of its illicit trafficking, gradually invading businesses, spreading from the coast to the hinterland, from suburbs to city centers, from Campania into the surrounding areas, even touching Rome itself (where, the press has speculated, one-half of businesses have allegedly been asked for bribes)—to the point of establishing beachheads in the North and even abroad.

Probably the turning point came in the 1970s with the establishment of the incredible Cutolo party—which gave rise to

---

[1] From Meldolesi (1992) *Spender meglio è possible*: 63-72.

the temporary dominance of the "new family" and the current fragmentation of the Campania Camorra into 113 main branches (listed by the Ministry of the Interior) with over 5300 stable affiliates. In any case it is clear that this worsening criminal pollution has penetrated even the sanctuaries of Naples' professional classes (such as the Rowing Club); it has crept into the city's most exclusive areas, where dirty money has begun to compete with clean. For the first time, it gives the impression that it can dominate collective life. Suddenly, in the winter of 1989-90, this expansion led to a wave of panic, and the danger of a new flight of "professional skills" from a city that badly needs to boost them was placed on the agenda.

In this situation a group of young observers—Ciro Coppa, Paolo di Nola (secretary), Gennaro Esposito, Tommaso Flagiello and Pierfrancesco Smaldone—began to meet regularly with Liliana Bàculo, Nicoletta Stame and myself for the purpose of bringing into focus a partial but faithful x-ray of Campanian criminality, a check-up inspired, clearly, by the compelling need to recover from it, perhaps in stages. What follows is a brief overview of this work.

The starting point for our thinking was the assertion that recurs often in the testimony of informers that the Camorra (the 'Ndrangheta, the Mafia) is an "overgrown power." This is why it seemed illusory to us to think of combating it with simple traditional methods of containment, or to address the problems of the South without explicitly taking it into account (as is often the case in current economic journalism). All the better then to focus attention on this major criminal emergency, even at the risk of exaggerating its importance and—even worse—becoming intellectually embroiled. In fact, while for the purpose of restoring the phenomenon to its actual dimensions it is sufficient to position it within the greater socioeconomic reality, the subjective aspect of the issue is more difficult to disentangle. It is no accident that the literature on the subject oscillates between cerebral theorizing and journalistic reconstruction—and generally results in condemnation and calls for state intervention. This probably reflects the tragic and compelling nature of the reality under analysis—the resulting trauma seems to allow only frontal attack or flight. On the contrary, convinced of the need to move beyond this dead end, our small group tried to take advantage of the daily experience of its young participants in such a way as to locate the phenomenon in a concrete setting, to gradually draw from it an inductive picture of collective life, to look in its developmental processes for ideas and avenues of escape.

This led us to the discovery of a new secret of Pulcinella. Any private citizen who really wants to can discover the essential features of the phenomenon without even reading the more or less official reports that are regularly published on the subject.

The argument is divided into three parts: what the Camorra is today, how Camorristi live (and how people live in Camorra-controlled areas), and how people might recover from the Camorra.[2]

The first of these is the least controversial. As is well known, the term Camorra means bribe. Extortion remains one of the basic activities of the criminal gang. When accepted by various businesses—large, small, and even minuscule—as a flat fee or percentage of presumed profit, so-called "protection" is a sure indicator of the violent power established in the area by the Camorra group[3]. And for willing young people it is also an

---

[2] A glossary on this is published in Appendix C of Meldolesi (1992: 163 ff.). Entries by Paolo di Nola, Nicoletta Stame, Gennaro Esposito, Liliana Bàculo. Ciro Coppa.
[3] It should be noted, however, that as with other aspects of the underworld, the bribe is also evolving. As opposed to monthly (or even weekly) collection, which still requires considerable organizational effort, some gangs follow the practice of serving themselves in "protected" businesses and stores (groceries, clothing, bricks and mortar, etc.). Others specialize in identifying assets and imposing a high

ongoing temptation, an alternative to work or stealing that is only impeded by the extortion practiced by other Camorristi. Indeed, for those who experience it in isolation it is very difficult to escape from—due to the life-threatening danger they are exposed to, the resigned attitude of their fellow human beings, and the action of law enforcement officers who prefer a quiet life. If these latter will not engage and people do not wake up the only real alternative is to leave.

But this is only one of the group's many illegal activities. Alongside it are usury (including debt collection for others), swindling (of suppliers, banks, insurance companies, the state, the EEC), gambling (which competes with *lotto* and *totocalcio*), cigarette smuggling, grand theft, exploitation of prostitution, and finally, drug trafficking and dealing, which is growing exponentially. According to an (undoubtedly conservative) estimate by the Guardia di Finanza, in 1989 the proceeds from this last activity reached a trillion liras annually in Campania, out of a total business turnover of three trillion. These are such high earnings that they themselves are producing a shift in the Camorra away from its traditional bedrock focus.

This is the birthplace of business criminality, that is—to quote Eduardo[4]—the "industrialization of dishonesty." Unable to invest money beyond a certain limit in illicit activities (short of opening the way *manu militari* into someone else's territory), the Camorra boss finds himself with a growing surplus of dirty money to launder and invest, partly in the hope of somehow legalizing his and his family members' future businesses. From being a strictly separate and parasitic concern, the Camorra begins to creep into the legal economic apparatus—

---

percentage bounty on their owners. This puts pressure on the latter to conceal such assets (perhaps by moving them elsewhere) and to minimize tangible signs of them, e.g. buying cars, expanding businesses, renovating business premises, or buying apartments. Even simply showing interest in buying a small house can trigger the deadly Camorra bounty....

4 "Vincenzo De Pretore," De Filippo (1975).

in construction, commerce, finance, real estate—thereby expanding the radius of its social pollution.

To follow the trail of this advance, we must mentally visit Camorra companies in the grip of violence, companies that violate the most basic union rights, have unbeatable unit labor costs, and make their way with techniques of intimidation. We need to get into the business fronts that cover up illicit trafficking, and the flashy kind whose purpose is to show off the clan's power. And into the category of grocery stores, markets, car dealers, clubs and restaurants, hotels, cleaning companies, small insurance companies, etc. in the hands of the Camorra. We need to keep in mind the professional circle it makes use of: the bank clerks, accountants, bookkeepers, municipal engineers, etc. induced by good (or bad) manners to augment their salaries in exchange for certain services. And we must study the corruption that moves the paperwork along in an administrative system encrusted with formal rules of legitimacy that can in this way be circumvented. Not to mention true transversal criminal syndicates—inside and outside local governments—composed of Camorristi as well as technicians and politicians who manipulate elections, snap up authorizations and public contracts, etc., etc.

As noted, simply focusing on this reality, perhaps with accompanying estimates of business turnover, court documents, and so on, generally leads to alarm and ultimatums: after all, it is this criminal network, with its infighting and savage violence, that generates the daily slaughter we are witness to. But the psychological shock ultimately leads to paralysis. So we opt for a different route: cooling tempers, getting the eyes used to the Camorra landscape, avoiding scandal (and unnecessary risks), and finally bringing the phenomenon down to its daily routine. It is commonly known that in villages (and to some extent in working-class neighborhoods) everyone knows everything about everybody. Thus, detailed information and analysis can come to us spontaneously, through our "participant observers": we can compare such things and think about them. This leads us to see that the rise of the Camorra, precisely because it is metastasized, sets in motion a whole social domain that is worth knowing about.

A MINUTE EXPLORATION

An initial reconnaissance had already yielded some results. We had learned, for example, that a recent tax provision declaring deeds for buildings null and void if they were not "regularized" by the building amnesty had forced the Camorristi to come out of the woodwork (i.e., to file amnesty applications for properties in the names of relatives and front men) with the attendant danger of falling foul of the Rognoni-La Torre confiscation law. And we had also learned that the defect in this law was that it put seized assets up for auction. Because in the typical provincial atmosphere, no one would dare buy them—except the emissaries of the clan itself, when the auction price became attractive.

In short, many signs encouraged us to persist, to focus on the particular problems of real life, to try to understand how Camorristi live and how people live under them. The first thing that tweaked our curiosity was (paradoxically) an element of weakness. Despite the seriousness of the present situation, Camorra culture in the strict sense is less solid and pervasive than it might appear. The very development of Camorra businesses entails a change in the direction of "gangsterism." Even language itself, family relations and typical rituals (of baptism, marriage) are rapidly changing—traditional rules of behavior (concerning honor, respect, slights, etc.) are giving way to the display of dominance through opulent and vulgar consumption—the Ferraris, big hotels, yachts, women, hundred-thousand-liras tips: a style that contrasts starkly with the modest dwellings of the original families.

And then trying to get inside the lives of the bosses and their followers, you cannot help but note the high degree of precariousness and risk. The bloody logic they live by is rooted in the need to face down the dangers generated by rival clans, their own acolytes, and the police. The deep-rooted desire for unlimited enrichment is in a sense blended with this absolute need to dominate the situation and with the implicit awareness that the next clash could be the last.

In the clan, of course, it is the boss who holds sway in the home (and over the entire family). But even here things are changing. The family endures as a pure sphere of affection among blood relations—but it is no longer the core of Camorra power, now that the arena of action has grown to the point of having to accept into the group people who are not relatives (real or acquired). It is not reasonable to expect respectful behavior from them in the event of conflict... And then, the Camorrista projects psychologically onto his children and grandchildren—they are the concrete proof of his ability to endure and are at the same time the personification of his aspiration to a "legalized" life. Paradoxically, their upbringing includes "no street life, unwholesome friendships, or drugs"— they must study, become professionals and (it is hoped) inherit the recycled riches.

On the other hand, this mishmash of neo-gangsterism, acquisitive mentality, and striving to become legal interacts with the social body by gradually brutalizing it. As noted, this is not the ideology of the Camorra group. Indeed, the imposed "protection" brings with it a promise of order and normality whose maintenance may even involve keeping petty local criminality at bay. This means that in certain periods, in view of the weakness of the social fabric, the absence of the state, and the danger of rival gang feuds, the population ends up tacitly accepting the dominance of a particular clan, in which case, to the outside eye, the situation appears normal. Nor is it unusual for Camorra groups to seek to legitimize their power—for example, by immediately paying out on clandestine lottery winnings down to the last lira (which are taxed at a lower rate than those of the state!) or by "virtuously" giving jobs to the unemployed (and subsidizing the families of jailed gangsters).

But racketeering discourages different orders and degrees of economic activity. Camorra initiatives (legal and illegal) gradually suffocate the social body and pollute politics. Creeping fear makes the fortunes of security-gate sellers and drives people to conceal even modest wealth. The violent climate transforms collective life, whose circle of hell clearly includes the drug addicts—I am thinking mainly of the young proletarian Neapolitans who claim to be "upbeat" and consider work to be "pointless."

Perhaps I should be more specific. The irreparable damage produced by the Camorra comprises a combination of very serious issues: small businesses cannot develop (and thus lay the foundations for effective social rehabilitation), young people—even children—are initiated into drugs and delinquency, the productive and professional middle class is intimidated and impoverished (forced to minimize its economic, social and political role), collective life and the democratic system are manipulated and gradually subjugated. And atop all this, area by area and gang by gang, the rationale of the drug trade asserts itself with its small armies of hundreds of men.

Can we expect to get out of this without a real breakthrough? Without a policy of law and order that declares war on the gangs by destroying their well-established headquarters? Without a profound change in Southern politics? Those who call for greater government intervention (usually to tackle unemployment) often do not realize that despite their intentions, increased spending through the usual channels actually increases the Camorra's appetites. Even here (obviously) what is needed is not "more government" but "better government," with all its attendant consequences (which I would invite *bricoleur* readers to construct for themselves with vigilance and patience[5]). The country is finally waking up to the fact that the guarantor culture that arose from its civic development has been exploited by organized crime for ends far different from those desired, and that the professional ideals of magistrates, civil servants, lawyers, doctors, etc. "don't grind much flour." People are beginning to see that the ministerial disease of (token) egalitarianism, laziness, and (backyard) greed touches and conditions law enforcement and the judiciary in various ways. It is clear that the government's increased attention to the criminal emergency leads down a path that will not be easy, to say the least, and which inevitably passes through a thorough re-examination of economic and social policies for the Mezzogiorno. [...]

---

[5] In the age-old culture of the South, what is said and what is meant do not always coincide, as we see in proverbs like "if you want to get along, complain," "passing a law shows the way around it," "thinking badly of others is a sin, but it often reveals the truth," etc. This suggests staying alert (and if anything, erring on the side of excessive distrust and a "what's really behind it?" dialectic) without evading important questions. For example—how to stimulate the motivations of the personnel in charge of law and order—dedication, professionalism, merit, pride in their role and service, connection with honest citizens? These are things that, paradoxically, seem beyond the reach of the art of governing theorized by so many contemporary social scientists.

Luca Meldolesi

Maladie d'amour [6]

Perhaps we have found the thread of Ariadne we were looking for. The psychological effects of Italy's troubles (even ahead of the economic and political effects) are more visible in the Mezzogiorno, but they exist in the country as a whole. Furthermore, along the way the horizon has expanded—from the narrow confines of public office to the Camorra group's range of action, to the vast and luminous expanses of the Southern condition. And the road seems open for a further advance.

In fact, the feeling of having stumbled across a general feature of collective life—noticeable in different areas, produced by the country's distant and recent history—can push us to search further for an answer to the question of why Italy has such a hard time spending taxpayers' money better.

RESOURCEFULNESS AND HARMONY

I don't know if the reader is familiar with "Battle of Ten Naked Men" by Pollaiuolo, which Joseph LaPalombara selected to exemplify his *Democracy Italian style* (1987). For those who have not seen it, it is a 15th century engraving composed of ten figures fighting among themselves, no holds barred. As the eye falls on the swords, clubs, and arrows—on the muscles straining with exertion or on the agony of the dying—the mind perceives that the whole scene mysteriously and ironically creates a picture of rare harmony. The intensity and even virulence of Italian social and political life—this is the American political scientist's metaphor—should not mislead us because in their full expression they have managed to build a vital system that functions according to its own rationale. This is a paradox constructed *post festum*,

---

[6] From Meldolesi (1992), *Spender meglio è possibile*: 101-120.

which certainly suffers from the impulse of self-congratulation to be touched on later—when Italians decided to abruptly change their judgment of their own country as the home of Monsieur Cambronne. But for the *granum salis* that it contains (along with the additional problems it leaves room for) I thought I would take it as a point of departure for the present chapter.

In defiance, then, of the political theories that have praised passive behavior and electoral absenteeism, Italy has demonstrated—La Palombara suggests—that a positive correlation can exist between a high level of political participation and smoothly functioning democratic life. It is a relationship that also crosses into the social and economic realms, probably flowing in both directions (from participation to democracy and vice versa), and has in addition a preferred "range," in the sense that beyond a certain threshold, it can become either too feeble or too forceful. Above all, LaPalombara thinks that the vibrancy of collective life has invigorated the way the country functions—social struggles have created harmony (an embarrassing proposition for those who opposed them). But little attention has been given to the opposite direction—that is to the fact that a *desire for harmony* might bring about collective action, and with it the country's latent political-economic creativity.

My proposal is to use the framework in its entirety—to put it to work not only to appreciate that over the past decades (in spite of everything) things have gone pretty well, but also to reactivate the positive process at one end or the other of the relationship when we find that we are (or are heading) outside the preferred range. What I am suggesting is that from the standpoint of harmony this is precisely today's situation and that, unlike the way things were in the past, it might be worthwhile to "love each other."

A cynical "law" of the human condition states that we are often fated to understand social processes only when they are on the verge of disappearing. Perhaps we have not come to the point of nullifying the relationship between vitality and collective harmony, but certainly something important has changed. Just when the echo of Italic deeds had reached the four corners of the globe (ironically), to us the situation began to appear in a different light. Much of the mobilization lost its spontaneity, many reasonable appeals fell on deaf ears. It seemed to us that harmony and vibrancy were on the wane, growing cold—and giving way to a much less "livable" collective climate. The first task, therefore, is to call to mind some snippets from the film we experienced as a way of identifying a gateway into the tangled issue.

We can begin with some beneficial expedients that have given contemporary Italy a leg up. These are tricks, unintentional effects, that have often disappeared because they were considered unpresentable by those who aimed to create a "decent" narrative of the country's history. For example, who does not remember that the struggles ignited in the cities in the 1960s-70s had the unintended effect of promoting development in provincial areas (especially in what has since been christened the "third Italy")? That they favored the decentralization of production and, through high inflation, allowed a negative real interest rate? That the political awakening quickly turned into an economic awakening by summoning to the forefront business leaders only recently emerged from obscurity (whether white or red)?[7]

And who does not remember how rapid industrial development exalted the mass entrepreneurial versatility of the Italian provinces, the family base, the small business, the industrial

---

[7] Among other things, this means that the vast literature on the labor market, political decentralization and the development of small and medium-sized Italian businesses, sometimes reported phenomena without managing to explain them. It was held, for example, that "cultural conditions" had promoted growth in the third Italy, but the economic and political pressures and inducements that enabled the exploitation of this preexisting humus were not studied.

districts—and the impressive wave of double labor that produced the country's sudden enrichment syndrome? And how can we fail to recall the new connection to Europe that was established in the late 1970s via the monetary serpent, under the impetus of pro-Europeans and a few officials and politicians, who managed to normalize (and ultimately render presentable) a country that was for so many reasons recalcitrant?

These and many more are the rays of the national "Star" that, for a time overshadowing the archetype of mandolins and spaghetti in mafia sauce, created a surprisingly positive image abroad—that of the ingenious Italian, capable of taking advantage of the most unexpected opportunities, proactive, playful and also human.

But in the late 1980s, just when this success had become clear for all to see, the European expansion of Italian big business was halted in its tracks. "The party's over," was the lawyer's sentence. Perhaps our technical solutions were no longer enough—think of the fixed exchange rate that stumbled and still stumbles over the block of "mysterious" inflation. Perhaps, some of the expedients had had negative side effects. This is true in the case of the mass media, which in its irresistible rise swallowed up the people and ideas of the social sciences. And of course, it is also true of the state's debt and deficit; and of public administration and public service.

Here we run into a larger and more serious problem. As the rapid transformation process forced businesses to restructure and change, something profound about the country's collective life was snowballing into an avalanche. The long wave of the revolution in expectations washed into the most remote corners, propelling even the most disadvantaged people into an unabashed pursuit of their own material betterment. The process of industrial diffusion across the land ended up marking time, while demographic trends, which together with migration flows had long favored the transformation, were now showing a troubling reversal. In fact, in addition to pushing many young people into illegality, the rush to riches led and still leads others to live on the borderline and persuades a great many to devise formally illegal systems for making money and gaining power. It also becomes an instrument of social ascendancy and here it spills over into every environment (including political of course), poisoning *pro tanto* the interpersonal relationships there.

AN UNEXPECTED ENCOUNTER

What are the roots of this powerful phenomenon? Several months after writing the first version of this paper I came across an illuminating page of Ignazio Silone's on "The Surprises of Welfare" (Silone, 1968). "Nowadays we are spared the sight of ragged paupers waiting for soup to be distributed at the monastery gates;" he writes, "but those little groups of petitioners one sees being shepherded by lawyers or party officials through the corridors of public offices are hardly a more edifying spectacle. No one would receive them, not even the lowest-grade party clerk if they were to venture there unaccompanied. In any case they could hardly find their way around in the labyrinth of red tape without some protection or guidance; not to mention the fact that they sometimes want this protection in order to obtain, not a right but a privilege, or perhaps even an infringement of the law." (Silone, 1968: 174).

One can sense in these few lines the complexity of the so-called political negotiation—a euphemism masquerading as a scientific category. The mass propensity to look to a "saint in heaven" for individual economic gain by offering specific remuneration (whether electoral or material) in return is a powerful conditioner of the political system. This is the basis of welfare dependency.

"To begin with," Silone writes (1968: 169), "the cost [of the welfare schemes] is far greater than it would reasonably seem necessary (...). The vast new army of officials required to run these services (...) seem more inclined to favoritism and corruption than civil servants of the old school – a fact which, it must be admitted, some members of the public are quick in taking advantage of." I was struck by this last observation because it is precisely the courage that I have been trying to summon myself. In my opinion, the root of the *conventio ad escludendum* on state instability that my reasoning began with is to be found precisely here—in the difficulty contemporary Italy has in recognizing the existence of a real, serious mass social disease that has taken hold in the population and threatens to engulf the entire country.

"Corruption," Silone continues, "has even got into the framework of democratic political parties and organizations, into their trade unions and cooperatives, and it remains ingrained even after the formerly underprivileged have become relatively prosperous. If one did not happen to be familiar with the kind of situation in which this sort of corruption is rampant, or if one had not devoted much thought to, one might simply ascribe it to poverty plus lack of education in democratic citizenship. Personally, however, I believe that these factors are inadequate to explain the present degeneration of civic virtue in circumstances of a kind that, both economically and culturally, are considerably less precarious than half a century ago." (1968: 170). It is particularly notable how the pride, modesty, reluctance, shame, and dishonor traditionally associated with the idea of asking for and even accepting help were later transformed into a literal "scramble for subsidy." (1968: 171)

Welfare assistance, Silone argues, becomes domineering "as soon as the masses emerge from their age-old lethargy and in one way or another have got to be kept quiet (...). Many people see nothing dishonest in stealing from the state; they feel it is like stealing from a thief." (1968: 168-170). But the running explanation of the corruption that welfare aid produces does not completely convince him. He offers instead the idea that "in the new type of relationship that has come to exist between the social-aid state and its citizens, (…) many of them lose their heads completely the moment they hear the words 'government grant'." (1968: 174) This is a valid point, one which in my opinion becomes more understandable in the context of the drive for enrichment that affects Italy to its core and obliterates an entire fabric of traditional behavior.

Thus, the phenomenon goes back a long way: it is a retrograde step that parallels the progress of much of postwar history. We are forced to notice it today both because of its horrific resurgence and because it has set a collision course with the further advancement of the country. And we discover that "l'Italia l'è malada," certainly for reasons different from those of turn-of-the-century peasants.[8] It is sick with cheating, with parasitism, with corruption, with crime.

A MERCILESS X-RAY

A person visiting the Mezzogiorno thirty or forty years ago would have been appalled at the violent way matters of self-interest were dealt with at the grassroots level. Alongside the settling of scores there was (and still is) an ongoing practice of leveraging the workings of the market to achieve dominance, but also even just to be able to get by. It is something that stems from entrenched social relations, widespread in different forms in other parts of the country, which, when freed from their centuries-old shackles and set in motion, carry with them a (ruthless and unconscious) rationale of unmitigated self-love,

---

[8] I do think it is true, however, that both the social conflict and the *maladie d'amour* that we are discussing are linked to the structural transformation of the *Ancien Regime* into modern democracy. Both stem from the crisis of traditional social relations and only decline when contemporary reality finally manages to prevail. In a certain sense they are both aspects "du même combat."

of affirmation at any cost. How can our memory fail to revisit the long post-Renaissance decline, or our having been until the day before yesterday (in the great majority) a people of lively gnomes devoted to agriculture, pastoralism, and the humblest of jobs—inhabitants of what once was a land of giants, as Fragonard and Robert depicted us in the second half of the 1700s?

If we look at the ancient homes and hovels in any Southern town, we may get the bizarre impression that they have been repopulated by people quite different from the original inhabitants. But if we look more closely, we begin to see a thread of continuity, or rather what at first glance appears to be an unlikely graft from the past that would never have taken root had it not been able to make use of the old social trunk.

This brings us to a general point. We are now witnessing the reappraisal of Tridentine (16th-18th century) Italy as a civilization of *otium*.[9] Divided at the time into small states with no real military or diplomatic power, our country experienced the commercial, industrial and technological dynamism of the time from the sidelines and concentrated its energies elsewhere. An oasis of relative peace in a Europe shaken by violent rivalries, it gradually became what Hellenistic Egypt was to the Roman Empire—"A Museum, a Library, a park of Archaeological Sites and Holy Places, a landscape for memory and meditation upon which the most cultivated and least agitated foreign travelers and pilgrims converge." In this way, "a great, lively and peaceful civilization, consolidated and stimulated by the successful reform of the clergy and of secular customs achieved by the Tridentine Church, devoted itself to the arts and to *otium* with extraordinarily fertile results."

I do not question this seductive reconstruction. On the contrary, I think the culture of those centuries continues to give our country distinctive characteristics that are part of its

---

[9] Cf. Marc Fumaroli (1991).

style and even its entrepreneurial successes (Vidal, 1990). I would only observe that the Italy of the thousand academies, numberless libraries, galleries, collections and assemblages of curiosities, the Italy of convents, colleges, seminaries, holy fraternities, cities of art and museum churches that attract so much interest today has also produced a downside. It complicated the process of integrating the broad majority of people who for centuries were excluded from the civilization of leisure and at the same time were attracted to a key feature of the lord's life: having money without working.

Herein lies (if I'm not mistaken) a deep root of the *maladie d'amour*—the national psychodrama which grew up over a long period in parallel with the country's development and (finally) ended up capturing the limelight. Unfortunately, the process is now at an advanced stage. For example, the term allocation ("lottizzazione") generally confuses two phenomena. It mixes up the "division of the spoils" (and in any case the accountability of state executives to political power) that exists in all democracies with the consequences of the disease. What does not exist elsewhere is the army of crazed termites that has eaten away at the tree of the state from below (and from within), and has conditioned (and promoted) the action of political and labor union leaders in an anti-meritocratic direction to the point of creating a truly alarming situation. One need only point to the notorious fact that an untainted public tender or job competition is like a needle in a haystack. Many of these are contaminated by pressures and referrals, others are rigged (although formally unimpeachable, their outcome results from an exchange of interests and favors), and some are actually sold.[10] And then of course once the position is obtained, heaven forbid you should ever speak of it again: it now represents a vested right, an annuity!

---

[10] It is not uncommon in the South to meet people who intend to buy or have bought, to the tune of millions, a government, government-run, or advertising industry position.

In Search of an Explanation

It is not easy to explain how all this came about. One way to approach it emerges in the question of why we are unable to properly focus on this national semi-Camorrist trend involving vast sectors of collective life. Convinced that it was only a matter of cranking the lever of material progress in the narrow sense, miracle-struck Italy had no desire to create a true autonomous socio-economic culture and imported the made-in-England economy lock, stock and barrel. But it is well known that such an economy takes as natural and pro-business the pursuit of self-interest without any restriction (except the law). So for a long time scheming behavior of this kind was seen as... "legitimate."

Just to be clear—it seems to me that the reality before everyone's eyes flatly disproves Adam Smith's (and the economists') proposition that it is not from the benevolence of the butcher or baker that we can expect our lunch but from their material interest. The truth is that we expect it from both their benevolence and their interests. This is a position that Montesquieu was well aware of when, in *Lettres Persanes*,[11] he described troglodytes as people whose material interests were not tempered and assisted by social harmony and solidarity with their fellow human beings—with social consequences that are not difficult to imagine. It may appear to be a real paradox, but the danger is precisely that of ending up on the very path of such troglodytes (with all due respect to this unfortunate group of people).

By putting together the economist's and the sociologist's points of view in a single framework, we focus our attention on the relationship between interest and benevolence in order to observe it from the standpoint of market operation. It is immediately clear that while the constructive attitude harnesses

---

[11] Montesquieu, *Les lettres persanes* (1721). Now Montesquieu (1964), p. 37 ff.

the rationale of the market, troglodyte behavior continually aims to subjugate it. While the former contributes to strengthening the social ties that make our economy work, the latter amputates them. From the mafia, corruption and the attitude of the Camorra to a thousand semi-illegal forms of behavior, and on down to freeloading, cheating and scheming, there is obviously an important difference in degree, but not in kind. In all such cases, instead of using the market for the opportunities it offers by forging bonds of solidarity with others, people presume to exploit the situation for advantages disproportionate to what they deserve. Generally, this arises from their perception of having been penalized by the "normal" operation of society and the economy (any cornered mafioso ends up saying that unfortunately there are no other options, etc. etc.). There is a real basis for this self-justifying black or white (or lion or lamb) ideology, but it falls well short of exhausting the vast spectrum of reality.

What I mean to say is that the relationship between self-interest and benevolence hides potentialities that remain to be discovered. When we manage to get past the nineteenth-century fences that still separate the social sciences, we first of all realize that the link between interest and benevolence (or solidarity) is *interactive* in nature. Certain parts of the country, once sleepy, have become enterprising. And at the same time, some crippling bonds of solidarity (community, group or family) have left the field to others that are more open. So that there is a rainbow of evolving conditions, and both the positive interactions and pathogenic aspects need to be studied from within them. For example, as a breeding ground for possible ailments there exists "in nature" a fear of utilizing market potential (just think of certain students who cringe at the idea of carefully evaluating their employment opportunities through travel, interviews, etc.). Along with many other specific and (often) contradictory states of mind there exists finally, on the opposite side of the spectrum, the aforementioned presumption to impose oneself on others through force or deception. These two extreme points of view, at first sight at odds with each other, expose an inadequate adjustment of one's behavior to the demands of the modern economy. They are linked to each other because the lack of confidence and trust in the market creates the troglodyte temptation, and conversely, the latter hinders the operation of the market. This is the two-sided coin that has kept us company on our Southern journey.[12]

Think of slow times in the Mezzogiorno, of that sense of helplessness, inability, distrust that prevails in young people—underestimating their own strengths and becoming lazy, knocking around with no aim. Isn't this, in itself—watching opportunities go down the drain like water—an important source of the determination either to get rich by other means or to leave?[13]

---

[12] And herein lies the root of the relationship, sometimes victimized vs. recriminatory (or supplicatory vs. opportunistic), and sometimes peremptory and aggressive, that prevails in the Mezzogiorno between the citizen and the state. After grasping this, I was put in mind of my first experience with this particular kind of duplicity (my first Southern shock, actually). Young and with hopes high, I had been catapulted south by my father's late decision to start a university career. My first day of high school I was faced with twenty or so silent and somewhat somber classmates. I was made welcome by a teacher. But there were those who thought my presence alone would make their life more difficult. On leaving, I found that my schoolbooks had been defaced with epithets. Group fear had turned into individual aggression. More generally, by this logic the modern acquisitive mentality operates as robbery—its aims are short-term, and the game is zero-sum, as in a stagnant society. But at the same time, such an attitude is established through rejection of traditional society and especially of the hard work that distinguishes it. It is a hyper-individualistic aggressivity freed from the old chains but unable to find connecting fibers in the Southern social fabric strong enough to channel it toward productive ends. It is important then to inquire into the education process and an eventual strengthening of these fibers.

[13] My instinctive perception of this danger prompted me to develop a teaching method that I christened "waking the sleeping dog." It consists of acquainting students with their abilities (however embryonic or ungrammatical they may initially appear) through short reports, speeches, writings, etc. on practical economic policies that affect their lives. To this end, topics such as employment, industrial linkages, development projects, the criminal economy, public and private happiness, or voice and exit in public services have proven (time and again) to be very useful.

The troglodyte temptation, unless it is identified, blocked, and then reburied, unfortunately has a high growth potential. Heirs to an ancient culture, Italians are very adept at manipulating the relationship between arguments and their effects. By appearing convinced of the goodness of their ideas, they can construct them (more or less consciously) to achieve specific outcomes—possibly by exploiting and exacerbating party, union, factional, or professional divisions. This way, following this double track—as Togliatti might put it—ideas that are *prima facie* defensible can lead to disastrous results. A small-scale test can be found in the many Italian towns and cities where local figures casually endorse a political party or even switch from one to another depending on their willingness to grant favors and bribes. Under these conditions (we should laugh about them while we still can) the significance of imaginatively blended political ideas is truly relative.

But the most dangerous potential for growth lies in the dynamics of the disease. Troglodyte behavior has mercilessly exploited the cultural and political development of the country. It stalked the great collective movement of the 1960s-70s, using its ideologies to its own ends by filling the spaces at the different levels it created. And it even served as the movement's undertaker, pouncing on the disappointment and the collapse of the ideals of justice, public morality, and freedom the movement had generously supported. It then got its claws into daily life by unfailingly placing at a disadvantage those who did not practice its iron laws of prevarication and illegitimate manipulation of the country's economic and social operations.

And here we come to a final cause of its spread—the knife in the heart that paralyzes those who consider themselves "upright" when they realize they are surrounded. Culturally defenseless, seduced by a certain abundance (and getting by), cheated by the operation of so many double tracks, those who have every reason to resist are generally not prepared to sell their skins at so high a price. They are often dragged along until the most serious symptoms of the disease emerge. Its sudden diagnosis can have deadly consequences. "What can a poor soul do" who has tried up to now to live with some decency in an environment that has been contaminated by such pollution? I do not share the implicit answer to this question.

How to Prepare a Comeback

And so, not least for the purpose of "mobilizing the troops," I suggest a consideration of the following points. First and foremost, it is important to understand properly, understand better. With all due respect to ancient wisdom, it seems to me that in this field grasping things thoroughly and getting ideas across with determination already in itself means changing things, putting the opponent on the spot. If as suggested there is an unconscious psychological reflex that comes from Italy's ancient noble (and semi-servile) tradition, if the bacillus of the disease is brought out in the open and is hugely invigorated by the drive for enrichment, and if it is reflected in self-denigration and a consequent temptation to abuse power, then we need to dig further into these meanderings to look for their limits and for escape routes.

The problem can be examined from the standpoint of the psychological theory of cognitive dissonance. As mentioned, this deals with the common relation *"cogito ergo sum,"* only in the opposite direction. When reality causes us to stumble over facts that disagree with what we know, thought-correction mechanisms may be set in motion to allow us to adjust. The country's accelerated development undoubtedly sparked a powerful collective psychological process of this kind (and at the same time benefited from it). One need only compare the endlessly repeated traditional behavior of Italian peasants of forty years ago with that of their descendants (in matters of economy, education, information, hygiene) to grasp the enormous significance of the phenomenon. But we now recognize that such a trend requires the gradual development in the individual of a capacity for change, and also—as we shall see later—a positive manifestation of will.

At first this dissonance can produce a negative outcome. If a blockage is formed, so to speak, in the collective consciousness, and interaction with the market and society has trouble dislodging it, the subject will react to positive pressure by dismissing it, while embracing what seems consistent with his or her own beliefs and behavior patterns. In the *maladie d'amour*'s mixture of modernity and archaism, this reinforcing aspect plays a central role. It is the claim that modern society should bow to a logic of violence that (more or less consciously) need not be abandoned at all—on the contrary!

This gives rise to a twofold, somewhat obvious consequence—the more pronounced the disease, the easier it is for it to develop, and the more relatively healthy society is, the better able it is to contain it. This will help us untangle another part of our knot.

Firstly, faced with the surge of criminality, most Southerners do not deny the evidence (as they once did) but excuse it by saying that the same thing happens in Rome and Milan. I have often been left speechless by such arguments because, differences in degree aside, they probably contain an aspect of truth that should not be simply dismissed as psychological antagonism. In fact, it is not difficult to trace our observations up the peninsula. Consistent signs of the same "duality of consciousness" are clearly visible further north in the somewhat hypocritical mentality of the Tuscan peasant (which I observed with the astonished eyes of childhood),[14] or in the joviality of

---

[14] Giacomo Becattini has written insightfully on sharecroppers and Tuscan industrialization (see Becattini, 1991: 25-46). I would only suggest that even that exciting historical process had its downside.

Emilia that often hides mischief, or again in the bigoted respectability of ultra-Catholic Veneto. And on the other hand, is this a surprise, considering that these regions played a leading role in the civic development of the *otium* we have been discussing?

Sometimes the truth comes out in exceptional conditions, as in the case recalled by Silone of a town that was engulfed and flattened by a huge mountain avalanche above a reservoir. Instead of being empowered to rebuild their lives, the survivors were supplied with cash in amounts they had never before known. "'The result,' said the mayor, 'is that in one of the factories many of the workers, now that their pockets are full of money, have walked out of their jobs. They spend their days in idleness, sitting around for hours on end in one or the other of the numerous bars that, since the disaster, have sprung up like mushrooms; or else they wander here and there trying to collect further subsidies; and meanwhile the factory is at a standstill' (...). In my view" Silone concludes, "no region of Italy and no category of its population is at present uncontaminated by this lamentable degeneration of the sense of citizenship."[15]

---

[15] Silone, 1968: 175. Cf. Cf. also the example of the Polesine flood and the remarks on Don Milani's Pastoral Experiences. The Catholics and Communists portrayed there, as Silone again writes (1968: 184-185), "are all cast in the same cloth, they are all driven by the same compulsion, they are all hanker after the same things, believe in the same values, share the same dream—to score thirteen out of thirteen in the football pools and to be millionaires overnight. Their concern, be they Catholic or Communist, is that other people should not think them poor. In the mind of the common people of Italy poverty has become a disgrace (...). Anyone having witnessed a brawl in the streets of an Italian city knows that the most frightful insult conceivable (...) the insult that leaves one no choice but to resort to violence - is the epiteth 'morto di fame!' - 'starved to death' ". As we can see, the change in behavior connected to the first Italian economic miracle takes place (and how could it be otherwise?) within a popular culture that for centuries and centuries was based on the dialectic between the prince and the pauper. And the mass aspiration is to lead the gentleman's life—that is, rich but idle, with no exertion whatsoever. (This points to an attractive opportunity—the possibility of continuing the dynamic anthropology of Milani and Silone by comparing their results with those produced by the second economic miracle of 1973-89).

So the problem is vast, and by its particular nature difficult to delimit and fight. If I persisted in chasing it in the Mezzogiorno it was so I could understand its concrete phenomenology—once it's in focus, it's not hard to find it floating around. Take for example the public reaction to the collapse of the regimes in Eastern Europe. "The problem," a Neapolitan railroad worker told me, "is that they only showed up for their paycheck. It won't be easy to get them to work…". And what about the various experiments underway in Chile, Mexico, and Argentina that intend to dispose of populist tradition and aim instead for private and public efficiency? And what were the real reasons millions of Democratic workers, including those of Italian origin, voted for Ronald Reagan? It is not enough to criticize the ultra-liberal ideology whose dogmatism had such harmful consequences in so many countries; it must also be recognized that contemporary historical evolution hides a little-noted problem that lies beneath it.

IS THERE A WAY OUT?

So, the thing takes on a new look. Up to now it showed us its pathological side—now we discover that it carries with it important opportunities. If we could concentrate our efforts on achieving good results overall in this area it would bring us knock-on benefits in terms of income and economic growth and improvements in democratic and civic life. And we could also promote our own and others' emancipation through what we accomplish—without preaching. After all, historically Italy has always been an international crossroads. In an era of democratic coming of age, it could play a far greater function than what is allowed by the public shambles it presents today.

But the issue is fraught with difficulties. With the spell broken that was preventing even a diagnosis, the problem of treatment remains. The presence of the disease in vast segments of the population leads to experiencing it on a reified level (attributing it to others and not to oneself). Meaning that it is also opposed by those who react against its spread.[16]

Yet the issue is perhaps less abstruse than it might appear. The generalization we have arrived at can be reformulated (fortunately) from a more encouraging perspective. To that end I would like to comment briefly on two episodes from real life. A Tuscan peasant named Del Toro, today owner of the land he works, head of an extended family and beneficiary of today's prosperity, had the satisfaction of tracing back his roots using parish records. He discovered that five centuries earlier a bull had escaped from a fair and proceeded to give its name to a peasant family—those "of the bull," [del toro]. Since then (and presumably earlier as well) the family had sought to bring about *in loco* the welfare revolution that for him finally happened. At the same time, a "self-made" Italian American, likely expressing a sentiment widespread in his overseas community, told me to "go ahead and write" that "it was the Italians who made America great"—a statement admittedly a bit jarring but indicative of his true feelings. "When they march in the Columbus Day parade," Gianni Riotta (1991, p. 72) recently recalled, "Italian-Americans are proud of the slogan 'America: we discovered it, we named it, we built it.'"

These examples allow us to observe the problem *in reverse* and arrive at a simple conclusion. While it is true that, along

---

[16] For example, those who assert the citizens' right to express themselves by referendum and local movements and prefer "home, wife and oxen…" are more upset with political power and party politics than with the inclinations of those in and out of government who are on the take (who raise rates, offer or take bribes, connive and intrigue, sleep at their desks). The parties, on the other hand, instead of separating the wheat of the protests from the chaff, are busy battening down the portholes and hatches. This means it is not easy to find valid and direct relationships between social pressures and institutional reactions—a consequence of the country's tradition of conflict, which is in any case on the way out. It should therefore be possible to gradually slow the game down and discover that democracy (just like government spending) could work better…

with the modern syndrome of acquisitiveness, human beings involved in processes of change carry with them the stigmata of the past, it is also true that the transformation itself can persuade them to reduce the effects of the illness produced by this explosive mixture. At the root of the ambiguity of conscience (between waiting without hope and a desire for domination) is evidently a legitimate need for personal redemption. If people are convinced, they "have a shot" (as they say in the US)—a chance, that is, to pursue the satisfaction of their essential needs by illegal methods, they may become more active and willing, enter into a positive circle of cognitive dissonance, and gradually tone down the temptation to impose themselves (without denying it outright). Once the goal has been reached, the feeling that they have "made it" lets them look back on the road they have traveled with some satisfaction.

So the results of cognitive dissonance can be negative or positive. Behind it there is ultimately the subject, who maintains his or her own discretion in the face of stresses, who allows one or the other of these preferences to prevail from one time to the next (and even alternately) (This is the so-called meta-preference thesis of Frankfurt, Sen, and Hirschman[17]). This made it possible, looking at Tuscany and the Mezzogiorno, to transition from one type of behavior to another and thus to indicate as alternatives policies that lead respectively to the encouragement of modern or parasitic behaviors. This also made it possible to feel astonished (up to a point) at the behavior of the Camorrista who would like a respectable path for his children. The truth is that, typically, those who commit themselves to hard work carry the suspicion that they could have made a more comfortable choice, so to speak, and those who

---

[17] Frankfurt (1971) "Freedom of the Will and the Concept of a Person", Sen (1977) "Rational Fools: a Critique of the Behavioural Foundations of Economic Theory"; Hirschman (1985) "Against Parsimony: Three Easy Ways of Complicating Some Categories of Economic Discourse".

instead embrace the illness feel that perhaps they would have been better off not doing so. But the goal is the same. As Southerners returning from northern Europe say with some envy, "everyone there is pretty well set up."

All this leads then to a peculiar hypothesis. Paradoxical though it may seem, the flowering of grassroots business ventures in the 1970s and the drive toward parasitism and lawlessness that we are increasingly aware of are offspring of the same composite social matrix. The epicenter of the former was the "third Italy," while the latter is based in the Mezzogiorno. The former happened in a period favorable to the expansion of small businesses, the latter in a less favorable time. The former—to return to Pollaiuolo—generated a degree of harmony; the latter endangers the legitimate aspirations of the country.

This is a hypothesis I find encouraging because it offers us an interpretive key for many of the issues before us—only think of the absurd struggle repeated at every level between the citizen and the state, between public and private. Think of the daily skirmishes pitting economists against politicians, the trumpets of Confindustria against the bells of Parliament.

I also consider the hypothesis encouraging because it ignites a glimmer of hope. If it is true—in Braudel (1984)'s words—that "the present is connected to the past, which shakes it, directs it, and goads it—now to dissuade it from even the slightest change, now to urge it to a necessary renewal," it is also true that the purpose of economic policy in the full sense of the term is precisely to push subjects toward a positive solution. Having identified the illness makes it easier to point to a series of valid measures directed at different aspects of the problem—as was indeed done in the areas of evaluation, civil service, administrative technique, and the Mezzogiorno.[18]

---

[18] Naturally this "joint product" of our line of reasoning might be enlarged through an examination of other aspects of the issue. (The discussion of minimum citizenship income, for example, which I comment on in Appendix B [1992, pp 151 ff.],

It is true, however, that these are "measures in search of an author"—they presume that faced with the worsening of the disease it will be possible to react. Here of course a tangle of national issues, of *puncta dolentes*, comes to mind.[19]

But behind it I see another problem. As mentioned, the spread of the disease (inside and outside the governing apparatus) mercilessly puts to use the factionalism that exists between political, trade union, professional groups (and the political currents that make them up). It feeds on cultural antagonisms that have had their day (Hirschman, 1991) but which, in the present situation, are probably the ally of the disease that is most hidden (and unconscious). Even while preserving the

---

was instructive). And what is more, for anyone insensitive to the gap between great principles and the reality of things (and—to be clear—surprised to casually read *Liberté, Egalité, Fraternité* carved on French public buildings) the opportunity for broader reflection opens up here. Despite the vehemence of the social movements of two decades ago and the revolution in customs they produced regarding family relationships, the role of women, traditional morality, etc., the way to bridge this gap continues to be difficult. There is the problem we have been discussing of aggression, parasitism and crime, no doubt justified in the minds of its protagonists, with the classic "for our family" (or PNF [*per la nostra famiglia*], as they used to say under Fascism). And there is the problem of manual labor, which was raised at the time by the young rebels of half the world. It is no longer talked about, perhaps because the break with the initial conditions has led the "freedmen" of developed countries to acquire the contempt for menial jobs that their overlords once held and which they now feel toward workers of color. This is a dramatic aspect of the current condition of Third World immigrants throughout Europe.

[19] To those mentioned above I would add the crisis of institutions that had been fashioned by the Cold War, the backwardness of parties faced with the challenges of an efficient democracy, the unpreparedness of a culture weakened by mass media and the influence of the disease on higher education. (Indeed, even in this sector the push for "massification" has not been accompanied by a new meritocratic order based on different areas of knowledge and professional levels. While in the United States there is a distinction between colleges and true universities—communities of professors, with advanced and doctoral students—and while in France the universities coexist with *Grandes Ecoles* with restricted admission and a number of public research centers, Italy has a diminished system that in practice discourages research and prefigures subordinate integration within the EEC. Moreover, its inefficiency is due to the "squashing" of careers, a lack of autonomy and a rule, let's call it peculiar, that allows professors to work "half-time").

necessary dialectic between progressive and moderate forces, it is therefore necessary to increase the *degree of harmony* among all Italian anti-criminal and anti-parasitic forces from different sides in such a way as to confront barbarism, and instead direct demands for enfranchisement toward beneficial ends, including the coveted "meeting with Europe."

Luca Meldolesi

The Three Scourges[*20]

1. Much of the thinking about our country consists of generalizations about the North and Center—the South as a less-favored area is towed along like a trailer, even intellectually.[21] Apart from emergencies in the media, its concrete problems attract little attention, either in the institutional system or in Northern (or even Southern) culture.

Reacting to this conspiracy of silence, I have tried to set my work outside the customary frameworks. I have come to the conclusion that a less-than-easy, sometimes spiky and deceptive reality such as that of the Mezzogiorno suggests more than other approaches the use of the research methodology of Eugenio Colorni and Albert Hirschman. The richness of reality—this point of view suggests—is far greater than we can imagine. It cannot be fully captured by models and statistics. For this reason, while the heuristic significance of such ingenious constructions cannot be ignored, the practical possibilities must be discovered directly through interactive work between thought and observation which, starting from the data, involves (and thus "penetrates") the observer as well.[22]

---

* This 1995 paper was "provoked" by a lecture I gave at the University of Florence hosted by Prof. Gabi Dei Ottati's course. Under the title "Scoprire il Sud" ("Discovering the South") it appeared in Meldolesi (1998), part 1, ch. 2.. The following text refers to the latter version.

[20] From Meldolesi (2021) *Mezzogiorno con gioia!*: 107-129

[21] To capture this point intuitively, it is enough to observe that talking about Italy without the Mezzogiorno is equivalent to talking about Europe without our country, or about the West when actually meaning the United States.

[22] *Ab initio* I should perhaps contextualize the decision I made when I began working in the Mezzogiorno. That is, not to evade my responsibilities and thus not to desist from a pursuit that for a long time seemed to me fruitless (like Micco Macco, the explorer in a nursery rhyme from my childhood who "searches, searches, and what

For a time, operating against the cultural grain of the region, I had to accept a condition of isolation—one that was nevertheless made up for by my American "opening" and the "probes" I was able to set up in Southern society. I became aware at this point of the intellectual opportunity presented to me to observe in full freedom something no one was willing to look at—the collective psychology of welfare as a salient feature of the Italian crisis.

THE RATIONALE FOR AN ADVENTURE

2. And so, in the mid-1980s, transforming my few students at the time into a research group, I followed whatever paths they wished to take. This is where the research on the Camorra, as an acute form of a more general pathology, got its start.[23] And from an observation by Paolo di Nola on the typical behavior of the Camorrista, to which I will return, I came to realize that even the most hardened criminals are torn between their own choices and the 'respectable' world they would like their children to live in. This small idea, explored in depth, reintroduced in different contexts, generalized by degrees and applied to multiple aspects of national life, made it possible to draw a *super partes* line of demarcation in keeping with what would soon become the movement "Mani pulite" (Clean Hands).[24]

---

does he find? Four python eggs..."). Instead, it happened that interpretive perspectives and concepts tested (and re-tested) in observation and dialogue with friends and students ended up miraculously fitting little by little into a mosaic under construction and thus becoming starting points for further learning.

[23] Meldolesi 1992, ch. 4.

[24] This is the Hirschmanian logic of the "petite idée" that needs to be developed, of the Chinese flower that opens on contact with water. The metaphor of the Southern voyage of discovery also finds some degree of correspondence here. It helps, in fact, in supporting the argument that the South is an intricate and complex reality; that in order not to lose one's bearings, it would be wise to follow a north star (the public interest); and that understanding the South requires an effort "outside the box," which means the bridging disciplinary boundaries and using appropriate method-

After this I realized that the path to understanding the pathological ladder that rises up from crime to corruption, fraud, parasitism, and racketeering had already been opened, not by the social sciences or postwar advocacy for the Mezzogiorno, whose best exponents were still incredibly blind to the reality that was taking shape before their eyes—but by literature. Or rather, there is one work that is situated halfway between the two camps: Ignazio Silone's *Emergency Exit.*

In the early 1960s, in fact, Silone wrote insightfully on the transition from the peasant culture of pride, reticence and thrift to the shameless pursuit of welfare benefits.[25] This "regression," as he calls it, marks the beginning of the high tide of welfarism— a euphemism that acts as a container for many iniquities and marks thirty straight years of the Republic's history—"les trente glorieuses," we might call it, paraphrasing Jean Fourastié.

3. Comparing my work with Silone's, I realized *post festum* that,

---

logies. It also clarifies my need to work "at water level," repeatedly questioning the phenomena encountered, and not backing away from their stark drama. Concern for the "common good," the meaning of the state and public morality are indispensable references for the present research. More than from a legal-philosophical point of view, they should be understood in an economic-social sense, from a concrete "policy" angle. This is not to be confused, of course, with a curious mental archetype present in the Mezzogiorno, according to which one should behave impeccably, but since this is "not of this world" ... many things become permissible. If nothing else—as I never tire of repeating—someone who steals an apple or fails to pay a streetcar fare cannot be compared to Broccoletti and Poggiolini! This brings us to a second problem. The public interest—and with it the collective need to consolidate and develop a true democratic market-economy society in the Mezzogiorno—must take precedence over political options. Indeed, the condition of the South is so difficult that, in my opinion, political forces can become agents of change in the desired direction only if they manage to put the public interest before their own political choices—thereby indirectly reinforcing the popular legitimacy of the latter.

[25] Silone 1965. His pages reminded me of my first election campaign. In the late 1950s, in Sicily, I was momentarily in shock at a remark that was made to me: "Handbills, all these handbills," shouted a sinewy man with raucous mischief, alluding to electoral propaganda, "Ten thousand liras bills are what you should bring us."

fortunately, I could distill the problem through concepts such as cognitive dissonance, meta-preferences, and the "maladie d'amour." I related it to the aspiration for abundance, but without working, which probably comes from the culture of nobility and its ubiquitous persistence in the South (but also in the rest of Italy) until just the day before yesterday. I placed it within the theme of Southern development by showing its severity, while arguing that it is by no means an inevitable evil. And, working by comparison, that is, by convergence and divergence, I gradually "picked apart" welfarism until I had transformed it into the other face of our reality, the one we would not like to see. Our ancestors (probably) already knew that only the fight against barbarism enables the growth of *civitas* (See below in the appendix).

In this way, I built my Southern experiment on the aspiration for a clean South that intends to rid itself of its ills.[26] But to achieve this result I had to contend with some negative tendencies present *in loco*. Self-delusion was one—underestimating the conditioning imposed by established ways of thinking—along with reducing oneself and trying simply to make do. These tendencies are summed up in feelings of inadequacy and powerlessness.

To fight effectively against this eternal "downward drag" I set about creating reference points abroad, oxygen lines that could tangibly demonstrate that success was possible, that it was reasonable to gradually raise expectations. It is a stratagem that has repeatedly yielded surprising results.

---

[26] Paolo Pezzino (1992: 9-10 and 24) called attention to a conference of Benedetto Croce's in 1923 on the Mezzogiorno: "Paradise inhabited by devils"— a saying that probably dates back to the 14th century. . According to Croce, "the 'reproof' that emanated from that saying retained, and still retains, relevance in its appeal to the need for a robust ethical-political life. In this respect, the ancient Italian proverb has not yet completely lost its truth [...] And in this respect, it matters little to us to research the extent to which the proverbial saying is true, since it is useful for us to keep it very true in order to make it less and less true" (Croce 1973: 85-87).

My Mezzogiorno can only arise from sustained, high-quality work, conducted with passion and intelligence by good people. Here Hirschman's possibilism, which unlocks thinking and helps to identify policy proposals and ways forward, has proved extraordinarily useful.[27]

4. On the other hand, what else could I have done? Current economic thinking was particularly unsuitable for the purpose. Based on the *homo economicus* paradigm, it inevitably eluded the very crux of the Southern question as I understood it—that of citizenship, morality. It was committed to macro analysis based on official statistics, imbued with powerful logical structures— neoclassical, Marxist, Keynesian—far removed from concrete perception. Finally, it was tied to unilateral, "pro state" or "pro market" solutions, and to techniques superimposed on reality: the overall plan, linear programming, shadow prices of cost- benefit analysis, etc. Paradoxically, this vast intellectual sam- pler, this mighty cultural machine built in 100 compartments, gets jammed in the face of... Pulchinella's many secrets about the Southern condition—the everyday truths, large and small, that too many try not to see.

Obviously, this does not mean doing without economics. But following Albert Hirschman's directions, we can fore- ground concrete individual and collective psychology and push the discipline in the direction of "complicating" it (Hirschman, 2020). Thus, it happens, as mentioned, that preferences turn into meta-preferences, the recommendations of the "optimum currency area" are turned upside down, and Scitovsky's *Joyless Economy* points instead toward a *joyful Mezzogiorno!* (Meldolesi 1990, Meldolesi 1992)...

This route also opens up the hunt for small- and large-scale

---

[27] Hirschman (1971). Cf. also Pezzino (1992), Capano (1997), Centorrino and Signorino (1997), Moro (1998).

solutions that address the need for the moral and material rehabilitation of the Mezzogiorno (and which should be disarm-
ingly argued, as if it would be possible to apply them tomorrow
morning). This playful exercise ended up bearing fruit by setting the coordinates of an economic policy scheme for the
South within which it is possible to rediscover a thousand
Hirschmanian devilries and stratagems useful for development: those related to linkages and linkage blocking, narrow
and wide tolerance, exit and voice, and so on.[28]

THE THREE SCOURGES

5. How do we set about looking for the Mezzogiorno? First
and foremost, the same way we go about discovering other realities, carrying with us the ideas we have formed over time and
being prepared to learn much that is new, even at the cost of
subverting what we thought we had understood. This iterative
exercise eventually leads us to certain points of reference that
are very useful in ordering information and developing analyses.

Enthusiasts of local systems in different parts of the peninsula have become accustomed to arguments involving contextual knowledge, forms of collaboration, and participation in
the life of a business. And perhaps also to discussing the industrial development of such systems in the light of Porter's
"diamond": availability and quality of inputs, the role of domestic demand and user sectors, market structure and competitive environment, the supplier-customer network. Clearly, this
way of approaching things has great relevance for the Mezzogiorno as well. But my impression is that if this path were

---

[28] My reasoning arose from this, from reflections on past experience and the need
to explain myself, and has behind it the fifth Prato meeting on local development.
It thus presupposes a knowledge of my *Spender meglio (Spending Better)* and of the well-
known contribution of the "district club" headed by Giacomo Becattini and
Sebastiano Brusco.

slavishly followed, much of what needs to be explained would be missed. The unique nature of the South would be lost, and with it the need to discover the Mezzogiorno (as distinct from Tuscany, Lombardy, etc.).

My inclination then is to turn to other reference points and to mix them not only with those just mentioned but with others still, as if they were color transparencies that become increasingly interesting (but never complete) as they are superimposed.

I think that in this way an objective observer of the Southern scene cannot help but wonder why it is that things are not as good here as elsewhere. Why, despite recent changes,[29] are we still breathing the air of welfarism? Why is there still so much crime around, so much influence-peddling, so much corporatism?[30]

Clearly the Mezzogiorno is no longer an underdeveloped area in the strict sense. The transformation of its predominantly agricultural employment structure into a primarily urban one, based on industry and the service sector, took place to a large extent in the 1950s-70s. There is, in fact, a vast working

---

[29] "The great turning point," as Bodo and Viesti (1997) call it.

[30] In the North-Center, we are only sporadically aware of the severity and spread of the "disease," which in the South, on the other hand, is palpable. But even in the South, most people lack direct experience of its acute forms, which makes it harder to decode the common ones that are widespread in the natural habitat (and unfortunately so many people are comfortable with). Coupled with the entirely Southern need to downplay the phenomenon so as to be able to "hope for the best," this creates a murky atmosphere that bursts open at times in the face of pathological flare-ups and scandals. It seriously obstructs the rehabilitation process. One way to overcome this opaque state of consciousness is to acclimatize one's outlook to the Southern criminal environment and then mentally reconstruct the contours of the overall phenomenon of the "three scourges." This requires nothing more than an act of will that goes beyond pious wishful thinking, because there is nothing mysterious about the theme. In a short time one can learn a great deal about a distinct, varied, ever-changing reality that bleeds the social fabric in so many parts of the Mezzogiorno. During the years of triumphant clientelism this concrete observation had the merit of opening my own eyes (cf. Meldolesi, 1992, ch. 4).

community in the South that produces goods and services, even though, for the most part, the size of businesses is minimal. The problem is that the development of this "nebula," with all the industrial problems it brings, has to reckon in a protracted and objectively exhausting way with a severe collective pathology.[31]

6. The war on the criminal cabals inspired by Judges Falcone and Borsellino and the "Clean Hands Movement" years has undoubtedly contributed to the country's recovery. But it is a task that is far from over. Moreover, it has not effectively attacked the reality of *ordinary* crime and corruption that characterizes whole areas of Southern society. The result is that the "liberation of productive forces" that might have been expected from the state's offensive has so far turned out to be very modest.

On the other hand, in the South, the security issue has to take into account the diversity and articulation of the criminal landscape. There are areas subject to the so-called *pax mafiosa* or *Camorrista*, where the criminal group that controls a given area represses petty crime, offers protection to the population, and leaves small businesses alone. Then there is the opposite situation, where gangs are at war for the control of a particular territory. And there are also areas infested with petty criminality. And finally, there are processes of evolution from one of these situations to another, criminal intersections, overlaps, etc.

At the same time, the fall of some major clients certainly has not abolished influence-peddling or clientelism—the phenomenon of interaction and exchange between citizens and the

---

[31] Indeed, the "disease" besieges Italian society in the Mezzogiorno from all sides. All local realities are forced to tolerate it; some are so afflicted that they take on a disjointed, disordered and pained appearance. Like a plant overwhelmed by parasites, productive and civic life in these places cannot react adequately—it is forced to adapt.

powerful that continues to play a prominent role in the life of the Mezzogiorno. Pushing for welfare, pulling strings, pursuing public employment, vote buying. These practices are still broadly present in differentiated forms and patterns, more or less severe depending on the situation.

Finally, an often defensive but no less serious phenomenon that exists in the South is the deeply entrenched corporatism of professional associations and trade unions, especially those that belong to the public sector. Along with clientelism, to which it is closely related, corporatism breeds a vast parasitic reality that weighs on the shoulders of citizens and works against the sacrosanct need for merit and flexibility in economic and administrative operations.[32]

7. As in any other democratic society with a market economy these "three scourges" coexist in the Mezzogiorno with opposing phenomena and behavior: the need for legality, the proper functioning of institutions, remuneration in accordance with work, etc. The difference is that in the South (but also in Brazil, Colombia, and other countries) the pathological aspect in its various guises is more pronounced, so much so that it cannot be swept under the rug. It is a question then—this is my view—of continuing to place it at the forefront and explicitly arguing that the issues of growth, democracy and social justice that we care most about cannot be addressed without clearing a way into the uneasy patchwork of contradictory coexistence between pathological and healthy behavior.

This is the case not only because the "troglodyte" option coexists alongside the requirements of the modern economy

---

[32] Probably because of my background, I had not until now found the strength to propose corporatism as the "third scourge." What convinced me was the absurd Petrobras struggle in Brazil (1995) and President Cardoso's reference to cronyism and corporatism as "demons" to be kept in check.

and the public interest in every person,[33] but also because the fluctuation between the two types of behavior that can be seen in individual and collective life allows a mixture of contradictory attitudes, we are often only dimly aware of to emerge in our consciousness.

It is possible to meet individuals far removed from the criminal world who are so deeply marked by clientelism or corporatism that they consider such attitudes and ways of doing things "normal," if not downright "correct." Or people who seem to be part of the renewal and the moralizing strain of Southern life and instead are implicated in episodes of corruption. Indeed, such a "mixed bag" is so obvious that at first glance there seems to be no way to get out of it. If you fight on the crime and corruption front, you easily end up falling into the arms of corporatism. Whereas if you target the latter, you have to guard against cronyism. And if you presume to take on all three, you at least temporarily lose the trust of various circles and feel like a lost voice in the desert.

Evidently, in a society that feels structurally weaker than it would like to be, the sense of personal inadequacy in coping with life continually produces a kind of "propensity for craftiness" that leads to a search for shortcuts to achieve one's goals.

Hence the discovery of the Mezzogiorno becomes a journey of exploration of such contradictions. We must examine the greater or lesser presence of these pathogenic factors in different local systems, the oscillation that exists everywhere between them and their opposite, and how economic and civic growth can be strengthened by intelligently utilizing the minute opportunities offered by these oscillations.

---

[33] As I wrote previously in chaps. 4-6 of Meldolesi (1992). See also my *Maladie d'amour* above.

8. In our game of colored masks, we need first of all to connect this "glimmer of reason" with the many things we already know about the local realities under observation. Here, fortunately, we arrive at a conclusion that is actually explained by a "mixture" of the two types of knowledge.

As we shall see more fully below, the hunt for Southern small businesses conducted by a group of professors, young researchers and undergraduates headed by the Department of Economics at the Federico II University of Naples turned up many more businesses than we expected. This has become so proverbial that when a thesis student complains about not yet having a subject to study, we tell them to look close to home— they can easily unearth an interesting manufacturing operation.

I think we need to account for these surprises—or rather, for the need for the camouflage that seems so irresistible to so many small businesses in the South. Evidently, it pays to do so—or at least, this is the prevailing opinion in a society that feels besieged by undesirables, often greedy for money: the kickback, the bribe, the recommendation, the freeloader, the bureaucratic fee, the tax for no real service, and so on.

There are typical expressions that reveal the existence of this reality, as when the entrepreneur claims to be a "man of the world"—usually an admission of a certain coexistence with "normal" forms of semi-criminal protection. Or when business owners claim to have done it all on their own, with no help from the state—which is often inaccurate but reveals a feeling of pride mixed with loneliness and despondency.

The consequence is that the social weight of productive settings is much less than it could be. Life in a great many local systems in the South is still dominated by traditional social figures. The lawyer, the notary, the magistrate, the senior civil servant, the pharmacist, continue to be esteemed and revered in their functions of representation and mediation between the pathogenic and healthy aspects of collective life, as in that of procurers of favors and privileges[34].

9. If we then go deeper with the analysis we have to adjust our vision to an extraordinarily rich sampling of different situations. To this end, we can finally invert the observational perspective and examine the success stories—the vital cores of the Southern industrial setting that we have been studying. Many of them can be grouped under the label of a local handicraft culture which, as in other parts of the country, has produced a fresh "boom" by entering into symbiosis with imported know-how, technologies and means of production.

Many skills involve products for the home and for the individual, as is the case with "made in Italy" in general. They may have a "refined" origin—like the silk factories of San Leucio, the ceramics of Capodimonte or the cameo industry of Torre del Greco—or may pertain to "everyday" knowledge, like the vast world of clothing and footwear. In both cases, the range of quality and price is vast and cannot be reduced to simple compartmentalization. Even the most common products are not necessarily poor in terms of quality craftsmanship, as shown in the case of firms that have worked for Valentino and Ferragamo, or that produce very expensive men's suits for the international market.[35]

---

[34] It is well known that in the Center-North, local authorities have often become activity-centers that can provide the network of production with efficient services and support modernization and restructuring processes in various ways. In the South, on the other hand, the private use of public goods and offices has unfortunately long been common currency. Public services for industry and local industrial policy have been halting at best. At times they have been conspicuous for their absence, and at others have resulted in actual harm (as in the case of bribes demanded in exchange for normal duties). More generally, the long pathological era in the South has left deep wounds in all local governments (starting with the regions).

[35] Unfortunately, the cultural environment of the South, often inhospitable to productive activities, can generate an attitude of undervaluing and sometimes even contempt for local skills. These create wealth, and they could create it even more,

And so the argument comes back to the pathological aspect. How much do crime, clientelism and corporatism influence the behavior of these enterprises? Of course, this we will have to answer on a case-by-case and area-by-area basis. But there is no doubt in my mind that in finding its way, an accurate reconstruction of the industrial processes observed must take into account the positive-negative interplay that surrounds such settings.[36]

This seems to me to be particularly necessary in the light of a second key feature concerning the industrialization processes we are discussing—this concerns (borrowing the expression of Ichak Adizes, a brilliant business consultant) "mutual trust and respect" inside and outside the company. The pathology we are talking about is produced by an acquisitive urge that is not tempered by collaborative forms of mutual trust and respect. As is well known, indispensable social adhesives such as benevolence, cooperation, and civility are in short supply in the South. Outside the family and friendship circle, individuals tend to assert themselves against others and not together with others.

This disruptive aspect exists in industrial relations as well as in inter-firm relations. Business practices that are improper, if not downright fraudulent, severely limit the full development of inter-firm relations and external economies and thus the competitive advantages that accrue to the group of firms through

---

but in collective memory they are often associated with the "toil" of the past—of the artisan, the farmer, the fisher.

[36] In fact, educated skills and everyday skills struggle in the Mezzogiorno to get started on the path of development. "And note," Matilde Serao wrote a century ago (now in 1994, p. 17), "that the elegant young people are the best dressed in Italy; that in Naples they make the most beautiful shoes and the best affordable furniture; that Naples produces the best gloves." It is worth mentioning how I came into contact with this problem. A few years ago an employee of my department asked me if I would like him to make me a jacket. I found out that he was a tailor who had been shaken down by the Camorra, had had to emigrate, and in Milan had become... a civil servant.

flexible specialization and versatile integration.

Finally, a word about the workers' degree of identification, their sense of belonging to the life of the enterprise.

To all those who have wondered about the serial closures of state-owned companies in the Mezzogiorno, I recall a paper by Liliana Bàculo on Alfa Sud in Pomigliano d'Arco (Bàculo, 1991). The absenteeism of the workers—along with their corporatist and rebellious behavior—undoubtedly played an important role in the lowering of this Southern company's flag, along with so many others.

10. To secure our ideas it is worthwhile then comparing the negative and positive aspects of the argument in a triple-entry framework.

For each individual local system, the framework asks what the effect has been of the crime, clientelism and corporatism in the economy, institutions and even within companies, on certain key aspects of the system—namely, on the harnessing of local knowledge and the acquisition of complementary external knowledge, on collaborative relationships especially between different economic units, and on the rate of participation in labor activity that tempers the inevitable divergence of interests.

These are, evidently, tolerated illegal intrusions that coexist with constructive behaviors and which, in case after case, prove to be more or less dominant. The result is the complex situation we know, where—as mentioned above—productive activity has a low profile and fails to perform the predominant function that would otherwise be expected of it.

The "three scourges" adjoin one another and sometimes merge into each other. It thus happens that productively, socially and institutionally, a company fails to reach the level of its aspirations. Hence the sense of "depression" so characteristic of the Mezzogiorno. It follows then that any conscious intervention must also keep in mind the impact (positive or negative) that it may produce on the pathogenic side of the issue.

11. This way of approaching the problem of civil industrial development in the Mezzogiorno is very different from the tradition we have behind us—from both the Keynesian and planning-oriented "Washington consensus" of the 1960s, and from the neoliberal position that came later. It thus suggests policies that are very different from those offered by the two approaches recalled, as well as from those related to them which, through processes of mediation with the Southern context, have long been used with little success. Simply put, we believe here that the local reality, with its specific characteristics, is the subject of the change and that it must be intelligently supported in order to strengthen the ennobling and enhancement of its capabilities and resources—a project entirely awaiting development.

If we want to find an interlocutor on the subject of the Italian Mezzogiorno, we should turn in my view to Manlio Rossi-Doria—his reasoning has long represented a very valid interpretive "background." Viewed in hindsight, however, it can open the horizon to a somewhat different perspective. Indeed, by interweaving the concepts discussed above with Rossi-Doria's geographic-economic distinctions, we arrive at two further diagrams that together with the framework above make up a three-dimensional kaleidoscope through which to observe today's Mezzogiorno.

12. In the first place, in its present formulation, the Rossi-Dorian generalization of "bone" and "flesh," still now the most popular throughout postwar thinking on the South, no longer

captures the present state of Southern development. There are hilly areas—in Abruzzo, Molise, and Campania, and along the border between Basilicata and Puglia—that have had a good start in light industrialization, quite intense in some cases. According to the technocratic view that prevailed in the 1950s-60s, the focus had to be on the productivity per hectare enabled by new seeds, farm machinery and irrigation—and of course on the economic results of public subsidies that built downstream infrastructure and industrial plants. But growth turned out to be a much more complex business. It is not by chance that we have chosen concepts for our diagrams that are difficult to measure by traditional economic techniques.

As the "philosophy of Artimino" teaches, the truth is that in developing a local system, practical, contextual know-how plays an essential role alongside the codified knowledge that can be acquired from outside. In addition, cooperation between competing units and employee participation in the fortunes of the enterprise are of considerable importance. And this means, I would add, that the ability to curb the "three scourges" is vitally important—this is the dark side of our Southern moon.

Now, such individual and collective qualities are not necessarily more prevalent in the plains than in the hills. Indeed, reading Rossi-Doria leads us to the conclusion that there are certain hilly areas in the Mezzogiorno whose collective cultural traits still reflect their nineteenth-century colonization, when the peasant and bourgeois effort to practice predominantly arboreal or mixed cultivation on very poor soils—up to 60 million olive trees and three to four billion grapevines—left an indelible moral imprint.

"This miracle," writes Rossi-Doria (1982, p. 60), "which developed around some centers of ancient agriculture already organized in this way in distant centuries, was possible [...] thanks to the assiduous toil and extreme thrift of the farmers, who worked hard every day, from sun to sun. But it is not only the result of peasant toil—[...] the role of saving, which was essential to these undertakings, was largely fulfilled by the landed bourgeoisie, mostly middle or petty, who in these precise areas, for several generations at least, had developed qualities of thrift, industry, and resourcefulness which they concurrently expressed in their professional activities or later showed in emigration. Anyone who wants to understand the spiritual foundations of the most civilized societies in the Mezzogiorno and their highest levels of intellectual expression should look above all where these peasant and bourgeois efforts were strongest and most constant [...] such that it could be said that trees and philosophy share the same roots."[37]

13. It is easily seen here how some more remote and wholesome areas—less affected that is by the "three scourges" —were able to find their own path to development after losing part of their population. They were not subjected to the trauma of social disintegration that has affected other hill and mountain areas. Instead, just as in other Italian regions, they have found in their peasant and craft traditions the knowledge and values necessary for productive effort.

---

[37] "Except in exceptional cases," Rossi-Doria (1982, p. 71) continues, "it is not possible for these areas to become true industrial zones or be suitable locations for even isolated plants above a certain size [...]. In this regard I would like to present an idea that has been nagging at me for some time, although I have not had the opportunity to collect any reasoned reactions on it from people in a position to assess its validity. The modern industrial world is so vast and complex that there is room in it for a multiplicity of activities, many of which can also be conducted based on small facilities or home-based operations. This is true even for some finished products, but it may be even more true for some specific steps in their processing. The difficulty of organizing them into small businesses and locating them away from large industrial centers is therefore not technical, but organizational." Rossi-Doria is thinking here of a designated "specialized organization" that would promote the large-scale decentralization of production, with monitoring, lead times, minimal administrative and fiscal burdens, etc.; but subsequent history has mainly highlighted the spontaneous market opportunities offered by small-scale production.

In some cases, these areas also benefited, paradoxically, from a twofold process: while taking advantage of the clientelist push for significant public resources, they were not front-row beneficiaries of the welfare.[38] This way, while in more favored localities, normally those in the lowlands, the interplay between subsidy hunting and clientelist handouts encouraged parasitic and criminal behavior, in the hill areas, often under less pressure (partly because their population is less concentrated), the need to make ends meet set in motion a more active mechanism of productive life that was a great help to them. On a daily basis, we thus witness the paradox that the most rapidly evolving local systems are not those traditionally most advanced. (It is a kind of historical reversal that can also be seen in northeastern Brazil where older colonized states, such as Bahia and Pernambuco, are losing ground to traditionally poorer ones.)

Part of the Southern hill country is now a viable presence that has managed to gain a foothold in a landscape otherwise populated by villages either deserted or sunk into torpor.[39] But then, moving down into the lowlands, the hard reality of the Mezzogiorno once again takes over. There are many situations

---

[38] More precisely, thanks to influential politicians like Gaspari, Colombo or De Mita, the inland areas took an active part in the transformation process in which extraordinary measures led to blanket distribution. But their healthier starting structure and the emergence of their traditional vocations probably allowed for a somewhat less ineffective and inefficient use of public money. On this point it is interesting to note how people with similar experiences can reach completely different verdicts even on the expenditures for the Irpinia earthquake (which, as we know, is an extreme case) depending on whether or not they belong to the areas receiving the benefits.

[39] So that some areas of the interior would almost say they had escaped the Southern quagmire. Many in Abruzzo would say they are no longer part of the Mezzogiorno. People from Benevento and Avellino do not feel "Neapolitan," while those from Molise and Basilicata look to Umbria, the Marches and Tuscany. It is a desire for "validation" that in the more enterprising areas indicates the acquisition of "Third Italy" behavior. In the more "difficult" areas, on the other hand, it translates into simple fairy-tale admiration: "There, yes, you would have a good life..."

in which living without crime on your doorstep is more a question of luck than a right. Clientelism and corporatism seem to be inevitable daily traveling companions. Even when citizen-pride collectives manage to lead innovative city councils into local government—this has been the case in Naples, Palermo, and Catania—they find that despite an extraordinary revival of image and functionality, the three cast-iron vessels cited create serious limitations.

14. So does this mean reversing Rossi-Doria's reasoning and falling in love with the "bone"? It does not. It means rather that, while maintaining the subdivision between the mountains, hills, and plains (in a three-way division suggested by the topography of the territory itself), the different local systems that make up the Mezzogiorno must be studied specifically, to understand for better or worse their secrets and possibilities and constructing—you might say half-jokingly—a "beef stew" thesis.[40]

In fact, hill country development, which affects a number of different sectors (from food, furniture, machinery, electronics, etc.) should not be kept separate from the vital hubs of the lowland areas. On the contrary, it is by strengthening and extending them that more comprehensive development could get underway, capable of involving still more people.[41] (...) In

---

[40] The development of the different areas of the South thus begins to look like—as I believe it actually is—the product of distinctive constellations of human circumstances, some of them accidental, which we need to be able to decode. In other words, the economic history of the area probably lends itself to detailed reconstruction and interpretation according to the microtechnological and possibilist approach of Albert Hirschman. In this perspective, the usual need for unambiguous, simplified and positive explanations is explicitly barred. Instead, we are after a complex of positive and negative factors, and their level of intensity, continuity and direction. Progress and setbacks often intertwine in the fabric of a current and potential tangle—that needs to be unraveled.

[41] For example—there are booming production hubs in the Mezzogiorno at the center of local systems differing in location and size, and often "encircled" by the rest. Then there are areas where the development of local systems is more decentralized and intermittent. In still others fairly widespread developmental

these contradictory realities, in their interstices and ambiguities, something seems to have been set in motion at last. We need to build more and more concrete "histories" of local and Southern systems that will educate us to detect such processes and identify their "emergency exits."

What, then—to tentatively conclude—is the moral of our introductory journey of discovery in the Mezzogiorno? The South is a very complex reality; it is a magma of humanity that we must learn to understand. It will be able to progress effectively only if this knowledge is accompanied by the determination required for a prolonged battle. "Italy will be what the Mezzogiorno will be" is a prophecy of Giuseppe Mazzini's that Manlio Rossi-Doria liked to recall.

APPENDIX: ON CIVILIZATION

Viewed from different angles, reiterated in different contexts, and generalized according to degree and area, the observation by Paolo Di Nola recalled at the beginning of the chapter finally gives rise to a general thesis.[42] The idea is that civilized and uncivilized behaviors correspond to opposite sets of preferences that coexist in each person's mind. The decision to behave in a civilized way entails the decision to reject uncivilized behavior, and vice versa. Someone who decides to be a mafioso is well aware that others behave differently. Indeed, they consciously (or perhaps habitually or by conditioned reflex) shun barbaric behavior. This has probably been true for a long time in our civilization—the ancients already knew that to

---

potentials are held in check and weakened by the pathology we have mentioned. And finally, in some places this pathology has taken over, replacing legitimate authorities in some of their functions and imposing its own law. Judging overall from present capabilities and achievements, it can be said that industrial potential would not be lacking in many areas. True, but of small consolation...

[42] Meldolesi 1992, ch. 6. An extraordinary recent account of the social oscillation between the two sets of preferences, concerning Catania, can be found in Russo (1997): 76-78.

establish *civitas* it was necessary to fight barbarism.

Such an affirmation takes us a step further since it emphasizes the relationship between the two sets of preferences and the need to act upon one to affirm the other. In effect, to develop civilized behavior, it is advisable to acknowledge and explicitly combat uncivilized behavior. Instead, the horror produced by barbarism often causes us to wish it away, to lower some kind of mental portcullis. This is probably the source of Southerners' need to minimize, their "inguattamento" (hiding). Hence the lack of interest, mixed with concern, of Northern Italians toward those in the South—but also of many Americans toward the Latino world. This can be seen at work in the integration process triggered by NAFTA. I would argue that a process of effective civilizing advance can be produced between the United States and Mexico if both recognize the positive and negative aspects of their respective civilizations. In short, it is not only the United States that civilizes Mexico, it is also true that Mexico civilizes the United States.

Uncivilized behavior typically hides behind civilized behavior. Few people explicitly assert the legitimacy of barbarism—even the most hardened criminals justify themselves by saying that under the conditions they were in, they could not have done otherwise. More often they are in denial. The Mafia, for example, was long claimed to be an invention of Sicily's enemies. Of course, behavior less serious than what criminal gangs typically do is easier to hide or pass off as legitimate. For decades in our country, economic and political corruption was justified behind the scenes. For many people, defrauding the state is still an everyday sport. The parasitic employee does not feel the slightest bit guilty. Scheming or cheating in certain circles (political, professional, academic) is commonplace.

So here we find different gradations of the disease. Falcone and Borsellino's strength was in the seriousness of the crimes they were able to target. Anyone who manages to push forward with their arduous work will have to attack the various pathological forms of collective life little by little. Surely it is plain from all this that such a path holds promise for raising the level of our civilization.

The bacillus of the disease, once isolated and examined under the microscope, turns out to be much more pervasive and comprehensive than it initially seemed. Just as the two sets of preferences coexist in people's minds, pathogenic forms of behavior (varying in degree, but not kind), are also very much present. In the early 1990s my line of reasoning easily made its way up the peninsula and was soon bolstered by the outbreak of "Clean Hands." The reactions abroad to these developments allowed me to observe first-hand the empathy and need for redemption in Brazil that culminated in the Cardoso presidency, the annoyance of noted American political scientists, to whom we owe the coinage "normal level of corruption," and French ambivalence between irritation with this "Italian" disease and recognition of how things actually are—even in France. Subsequently, attention to corruption took wing, involving the International Monetary Fund and the World Bank and bringing to the forefront the issue of "transparency" in domestic and international economic behavior—an issue that has fortunately found much support in the United States. All this has bolstered my general thesis. Further civilizing in the sense of furthering economic, civic and democratic development needs to look pathological behavior in the eye and fight it.

Obviously, the presence of the two sets of preferences entails the possibility of moving from one to the other. Politicians who began their careers for noble reasons can become cynics and criminals. When I was a boy in Sicily it was said that Catania had no mafia and that Messina, Syracuse and Ragusa were "babbe" provinces—i.e., stupid... Later, unfortunately, things changed. By contrast, the area around Castellammare di Stabia was long dominated by the d'Alessandro clan, but political, social and even personal events among the gangsters led to the clan's dissolution. Similarly, after the capture of the big mobsters in Palermo and the fall of the big politicians in Naples, people in the two "capitals" of the Mezzogiorno were finally breathing different air. The problem continues to be what can be done to consolidate such successes and push society in the desired direction?

PART IV

Education and Beyond

Luca Meldolesi

Amorous Bumblebee, Where Are You Headed?[1]

1 – When what we are doing begins to feel "risky," I think the time has come to pick up the thread again and look into possible solutions, however modest. (...) We need to understand and articulate our thinking and make judicious use of our small steps forward (*adelante*, Pedro!).

With this in mind, I would like to start out with Giacomo Becattini's metaphor of the bumblebee (Inaugural lecture, Artimino 1995, on "Local systems as interpretive tools for Italian development"). "Italy," he says, "is the bumblebee of Europe, a country that always seems about to plummet to the ground, but which, at the last moment, with a skillful, unexpected, upward thrust, takes flight again." The reason for this, as I understand it, is meant to be sought in local manufacturing systems made up of small and medium-small businesses, in an intricate and widespread labor market affected by industrial dwarfism and distinctive specialization.

Is this true or not? It seems to me at the same time both more and less true than Becattini and Brusco have told us up to now. It is truer because the attraction and sympathy for local systems (and the "districtist" literature) is not due solely to the productive achievements or the social empowerment enabled by small-scale production—our friends' warhorses. There is more to it than that: one gets the impression that such realities represent a kind of crucible for the future Italy—a more genuine, democratic and prosperous Italy that opposes both marginalization and the establishment. One more step takes us

---

[1] From *Italia Vulcanica* n. 3 (2019): 27-35

to the point—to a modern Italy that represents an alternative to everything that smacks of the parasitic, aristocratic and feudal at every level of the social pyramid.

And here we also see why Becattini and Brusco's reasoning is less true than they suggest. It is not only local systems that keep the bumblebee in the air. The task of the intellectuals cannot be just to support and amplify such experiences. Instead, it seems essential to me to understand both why the bumblebee tends to crash and why it recovers. In the extraordinary fabric that makes up our country from the island of Lampedusa to the Brenner Pass, the forces of democracy and the market economy (and thus of equality of opportunity, merit, labor, etc.) unfortunately coexist dramatically with a "feudal" and pathological reality, one that we have spoken of many times. It was not by chance that our argument at Artimino centered on this point. Without being able to identify and combat the negative pole (including recommendations, favoritism in public contracts and professorships, and so on) you cannot effectively advance on the positive side.

Our gamble therefore is on finding concrete interconnected solutions that make this path viable. For now, at least, the bumblebee is not a caterpillar turning into a butterfly. Despite the "divine surprise" of "Clean Hands," we are far from the finish line and must be equipped to succeed in a difficult endeavor. It is not enough for us to be simply good people, or even isolated Cassandras. We need to experience the future in the present—that is, to support the flight of modern, civilized Italy on a daily basis.

Unfortunately, the reality of the situation is highly complex. Positive and negative are mixed in politics, the economy, society, and the family. Moreover, we live in the least stable area when it comes to modernity. We cannot place our work in the framework of the "red region," as our friends do. It is crucial for us to preserve our orientation and move forward.

From the beginning, partly because of university feudalism, we have sought solutions across a broader spectrum—in both study and work. Much research and much activity can be pursued in such a way as to favor the flight of the bumblebee. Our ambition is gradually to create a network of diverse people able to play meaningful roles in this process. It is a delicate task that we have only recently begun, but it represents a true outgrowth of our collective life—an outgrowth that can expand from the South to Rome and to the North, and vice versa, as a tool for eliciting change.

It is painstaking and complex construction work, and it unfolds from the bottom up and from the top down. This last aspect is especially important. The well-established people we are interested in are often overworked and locked into their own specializations. In order to engage them and bring them out of isolation, it is necessary to offer them high quality input—and then figure out how to "cook the omelet." It is a mistake to get too close and risk being sucked in, and to stay too far away and lose contact. You have to be able to invent a team game between general orientation and qualitative and quantitative contributions. This is what we have begun to experience.

One final word on the problem of politics. Our center-left orientation is not closed *a priori* to the right and has a number of reservations about the feudal aspects of the left. For this reason, seizing the moment for propagandizing does not suit our purposes. Rather, we must be able to find ways forward by staying close to the "technicians" (as Albert once told me). And to do that, the point of reference is the public interest.

2 – We can look at the question from a different angle. From the point of view of an "uncommonly restless spirit"—as a nursery rhyme from my childhood said of Hamlet—the problem takes

on a very special significance. It is in fact true that independence of thought, an instinctive revulsion at any sort of university intrigue, and a de facto distance from "professional" work have predisposed me to a somewhat circumscribed experience. "But who gave you tenure?!" exclaimed a professor friend to whom I had expressed my true feelings. Indeed—as you often say— Nicoletta and I are very unusual academics. Someday we'll tell you the story.

For now, you'll have to settle for the consequences, which are well known. The environment disturbed by such heresy creates a fairly visible antiseptic cordon around it. While it is easy for me to converse with colleagues from the world's most prestigious universities, in Rome and later in Naples, I found myself isolated and virtually without influence inside the university. The result is that from the outside I must appear to be a specialist in young people's issues—that is, concerning that period so dear to Michel Crozier that runs from the end of public school to the beginning of working life. This "phase," which according to Marcello de Cecco is particularly demarcated and segregated in our country, for me on the contrary represents a privileged interval—in the sense that I gladly interact specifically with young people between the ages of 20-25 and 30-35.

Later on, of course, they look for work and everything seems to once again fall back into its natural cycle, without developing further. Fortunately, this is not quite the case: "the principle of conservation and mutation of social energy" allows for a different pathway, circuitous but interesting. Having become professsionals, my students and friends may once again take an interest and renew the conversation. Every time this happens, I see that I have not been wrong to live a life that is not biodegradable in the Italian landfill. To my great delight, today I could simply be a covert adviser to the many good technicians I know (or can get to know) in the central and peripheral structures of the state and the economy.

But the fact is, we have ended up together nurturing another project. Instead of a two-stage solution—learning and then maturity—it is perhaps possible to create a continuum that links old students with new ones in the context of a more stable connection. The driven professional condition my ex-students move in makes a non-episodic commitment difficult for them. The younger people, on the other hand—the students—have a more collective spirit. Their inclusion—as Paolo di Nola rightly says—is already a form of coordination. We then have to work toward achieving more of it. Again, difficult but not impossible!

A second reason for setting things up this way is social in nature. Our best students from the 1970s, like Filippo Bucarelli and Paolo Giacomelli have in a certain sense been uprooted because they come from the pneumatic vacuum of the Roman middle classes. Giving them a stable link with young people from the South can make them more practical and useful ("Rome," as I wrote in "Mezzogiorno Perduto e ritrovato", 1996, "is a little bit of everything"; which also means we must be careful that it is not so little that it is nothing at all!).

Here therefore the relationship reverses and begins to create an interesting feedback loop. If things work out, our contribution to the bumblebee's flight will grow. It will no longer only produce antibodies against the most common and stubborn Italian diseases but will also become a task of escorting the bee's upward flight in the periphery-center-periphery relationship (and then hopefully, South-North-South as well). Here the two experiences we are following have already yielded surprising results. In fact, just reflect on the relationship between the core "100 projects" group and the subjects that have been rewarded and reported—Filippo is already talking about a national current of our own (!). The same goes for the Act 44/86—Paolo Giacomelli's inclusion should result in a central hookup for all our local initiatives (Maurizio's, the book, Gragnano's, perhaps even Gianni's). Something therefore seems to be stirring.

But to develop in a positive direction this something should take care to maintain a certain (optimal) imbalance between various relationships: internal-external, Rome-Naples, North and South, etc. One example will suffice. The Bucarelli issue came up *after* the meeting with Brazilian ministers in late September—that is, after Nicoletta and I had shown that we could "dominate the game" (and now we are going to Reggio Emilia with Catherine Grémion and Filippo for the same reason). This suggests moving by means of "nets and knots," meaning that we need to cast the nets and then tighten the knots and vice versa. Hence the need to alternate primary commit-ments following this logic of imbalance in which each step forward induces the next (but without falling into the 'one thing at a time' trap!).

In conclusion, beginning this new venture is not easy. But there is very great scope for upgrading the state and economy of the country, and an enormous amount of positive energy is required both at the center and in the regions, provinces and local systems. Our problem is understanding how to fit into this current in a coordinated way and how to advance it by freeing it from the countless elements of feudal conditioning in Italy, which unfortunately reproduce themselves in extraordinary abundance. I have confidence in everyone's ability. And in your spirit of adventure!

Dedicated to Mita and Walter

Luca Meldolesi

A Need to Split in Two[2]

Let me quickly put down on paper some key points concerning our experience that I have just discussed with Mita.

1) When I speak of us as a "tribe of improbables" I do so *pour cause*. At least as far as intentions go, what I'm referring to is a stable condition of life that could naturally be expanded over time through interaction with a wide variety of experiences. (To test the idea, I randomly inserted it in a class where we were talking about women, families, singles, etc.).

2) But when I speak of "tribes," what I have in mind is the American approach. The eccentric, genius professor is sometimes allowed to set up shop out in some remote prairie so that he can do whatever he wants—and it will clearly be impossible to get up to any mischief.

3) It is not out of the question that this was the reasoning of whoever it was that sent me from Rome into exile in Cosenza 15 years ago. It seems clear to me now that their calculations were incorrect since, also thanks to Augusto Graziani, Albert Hirschman, and now Giacomo Becattini, my and our influence has gradually established itself. For example, despite the hustle and bustle, the prospects arising from Grumo Nevano seem on the whole to be encouraging.

4) However, it is also true that we are not yet able to fully face up to "moving off the reservation," when it comes to entering the world of work. Except for Maurizio, those who are working (like Gianni or Stefania) say that the possibility of incorporating our message into their business is quite limited.

---

[2] From *Italia Vulcanica* n. 3 (2019):67-68

Yet, with the placement of Mita, Paolo and Walter in Rome, an important phase of experimentation *in corpore vili* has begun, which I am following closely.

5) I have been experiencing for days a strong need to split in two. On the one hand I feel I need to be fully myself in order to continue with the construction of our perspective; on the other I feel I should identify with the needs of Luca Lo Schiavo, Filippo Bucarelli and Paolo Giacomelli. I am trying to understand their doubts, their defensive reactions. I am trying to see the world through their eyes—above all the world of the office, of operations, bureaucracy, etc. I think Mita, Paolo and Walter have to enter into this line of thinking and spiritual exercise so that they can be at the same time—as I said to Mita—model officials... and model rebels.

Luca Meldolesi

Development Chains[3]

In order to release the excerpts from the Second Conference on Albert Hirschman's Legacy, *A Bias for Hope* (Meldolesi, Stame, eds., 2019), Nicoletta and I had to slog through the usual (multiple) proofreads. But it was also an inadvertent opportunity to reconsider, all together, the collected texts (from the October 2018 meeting in Washington D.C. at the World Bank)—particularly those that had development as their dominant theme.

As known, this issue did not emerge until after World War II—first as development economics (a subdiscipline of economics) and then as development in general, *tout court*. Even after the topic had fallen out of fashion in the American universities, interest in development survived if for no other reason than because it affects a large segment of humanity—so that in a sense the World Bank represents an important preserve of it, one might even say a sanctuary…

In any case, having reread the papers I posed the question—what had I learned that was new?

Of course there were many things: numerous facts, theoretical observations, etc. But one thing struck me above all. It is an "absence" rather than a presence. That is to say, the idea is no longer in circulation today of the "chain of development" that must inevitably unfold over time—or perhaps there is only the odd glimpse of it in reference to development projects (such as Albert's observation that monitoring the progress of a project requires a journey of discovery into numerous realms, from the technological to the political).

---

[3] From Meldolesi (2018), *Eppur si può*: 226-231.

159

I think that this kind of "theoretical navigation" needs to be reintroduced organically so that it can be generalized.

In other words, many have completed one part (thought and/or action) of the trajectory of a given course of development—the part that was generally to their liking (or within reach). But then they would leave to others the task of following through with the trajectory, and sometimes it is not clear that it happens at all. So it is not unusual to encounter particularly interesting results that are, however, partial—perhaps useful only as inspiration for new initiatives elsewhere...

It does not appear to me in doubt that this is the way things are—if only because "nobody" on their own is able to complete the entire "journey." We too, like those we are addressing, have a specific occupation that focuses on one aspect rather than another of the overall issue—we are teachers, civil servants, managers, professionals, entrepreneurs, etc. But the difference in our case is that we are the ones who "explicitly posed the problem," and we can detect the "deficiency" in how it has been addressed—which is precisely what happened to me while I was correcting the drafts of the Second Conference.

In saying this I certainly do not mean to exaggerate our role—we are by no means getting ahead of ourselves. We have learned a great deal from Hirschman and other great development thinkers, and on the practical level as well we know that we still have much, much to learn. Simply put, the point is that the issue exists, and our experience suggests to us some small observations, and perhaps some remedies suitable for the purpose.

Take, for example, "the principle of the conservation and mutation of social energy." (Hirschman, 1984). Obviously, this presupposes the existence of social energy—think of 1848, of the Resistance, of the Cultural Revolution, of 1968 (to name but a few movements, spontaneous and or provoked, that have been epoch-making). Albert observed that after taking part in a great mass movement, many individuals retain their energy and then reuse it, perhaps even in another field (such as economics versus politics).

It is an analytical observation that I think is insightful; but nevertheless, it is not enough, in my opinion, for those who intend to suggest policies appropriate to it.

In the first place because such energy may be *in potentia*, in which case there is still the large problem of setting it in motion. And also, because once such energy is reawakened it is possible to try to reproduce it in successive waves—as long as the initial constellations of circumstances continue to exist, or it is possible to bring other circumstances to a head that are relevant to the task at hand (as the Mazzinian heroes of the Risorgimento tried to do). And finally, because the orientation and direction of movements is still a problem—in the sense that, in the "shifting involvements" of life, there are those who retreat disappointed from the scene, those who conserve their energy for later reuse, and still others who try to continue *sic et simpliciter* on the path they have taken, perhaps by other means.

Which is to say, "[...] the principle of the conservation and mutation of social energy" certainly does not exclude the existence of its opposite—that is, of people who are committed to galvanizing such energy and causing it to evolve positively by directing it toward the desired and shared goals.

Development chains can take a thousand forms, and a thousand more can be invented—usefully. I assume, as mentioned above, the existence of energies that promote their own implementation and thus their reformulation (cultural, economic, political, etc.). What is more, these sequences can influence each other and interact, because positive processes occurring in one development chain can easily migrate into others. Not to mention, finally, that assessments of their operation change significantly depending on who is expressing them, whether the initiator, the user, those who evaluate them in terms of political consensus, and so on.

On the other hand, that development requires chains of elaboration and implementation is simply an observation. Every private and/or public project requires them—from the most abstract and general to the most specific and circumscribed. But I find inappropriate, for example, the widespread use of the expression "chain of command," which is actually derived from military jargon. Because these are complex processes involving multiple actors and proceeding gradually over time, and what is more, the democratic aspect of the issue is by no means secondary. And finally, it is a fact that each link in the chain (from the first to the last) has its own value—such that its contribution with respect to the goal can be decisive.

It is true, on the other hand, that a great deal of energy is transferred (or not) from one link to another—in the sense that, just as Albert Hirschman taught us, it resides and is activated at the point of passage (from link to link in the same chain, or transversely, across different chains), so that it can inject the necessary stimulus. It can also be too strong, too weak or nonexistent. It is therefore necessary to learn how to manage these many junctures—as Paolo di Nola's private-public management experience shows.

More generally, questions concerning development evolve over time. Periods of mobilization alternate with periods of rest (which are often more extended than the former). There is thus a major problem of "continuity" (among those who share its civilizing aim: growth, democracy, freedom, social justice, etc.). There is a problem of containment (with respect to tendencies to dispersion), and there is the flame that needs to be fanned. And the "social grounds" for the network itself need to be continually reactivated—not least because employment along with personal and generational reasons might suggest otherwise.

It is necessary therefore to invent an "art of staying together" that progressively renews, in thought and action, both individual and collective interest in the problem of development, and which is not only able to replicate it in different sectors and territories around the world, but will relentlessly interrogate the horizons of the possible and can concretely promote the opportunities it finds—on a small and large scale.

This is indeed a purpose of our Colorni-Hirschman International Institute—an institute which is organizationally minimal, but which, by placing itself at the service of the Hirschmanian diaspora in different parts of the world, has in fact carved out a small role for itself—in proposing and re-proposing (in theory and in practice) development issues.

Inevitably, we offer first and foremost what we have done so far and what we are today—a "circle" that was formed at the university and found a way to expand into many quarters of the Mezzogiorno. It shaped several intellectuals and trained many practitioners, facilitating their access to certain private and public nerve centers so that they could inject a breath of fresh air, of competent rebellion…

Experience shows that this can indeed make a difference (for the resuscitation of lifeless situations, as well as for unleashing bold impulses for the future), and that it still represents a concrete alternative to the diasporic process of disintegration that is unfortunately underway. And which, it must be recognized, would inevitably be followed by an eclipse—of unknown length—of the very development problem that has up to now illuminated our path...

BIBLIOGRAPHY

BIBLIOGRAPHY

Italia Vulcanica 1, *Qui comincia l'avventura.* 2018. Roma: IDE.
Italia Vulcanica 2, *L'alta marea, cronache dall'Italia vulcanica.* 2019. Roma: IDE.
Italia Vulcanica 3, *Il Mezzogiorno della speranza.* 2019. Roma, IDE.
Italia Vulcanica 4, *Mal di crescita.* 2020. Roma: IDE.
Italia Vulcanica 5, *Bingo!* 2020. Roma: IDE.
Italia Vulcanica 6-7, *Montagne russe.* 2020. Roma: IDE.
Italia Vulcanica 8, *Avant le deluge.* 2020. Roma: IDE.
Italia Vulcanica 9, *Napoli oh cara.* 2020. Roma: IDE.
Italia Vulcanica 10, *Dall'alto della Cabina.* 2021. Roma: IDE.
Italia Vulcanica 11, *La montagna e il topolino.* 2021. Roma: IDE.
Italia Vulcanica 12-13, *Il coraggio dell'innocenza.* 2022. Roma: IDE.

Bàculo, L. (1991) "Organizzazione produttiva e grado di inefficienza
nelle aree sottosviluppate. Il caso dell'ex-Alfa Sud di Pomigliano".
In *Rassegna Economica*, n. 3.
Becattini, G. (1991) "Crisi e sviluppo dell'economia toscana dal 1945
al 1963. Temi rilevanti e problemi aperti" in *La Toscana nel secondo
dopo guerra*,eds. L. Ballini, L. Liotti and M. Rossi. Milano: Franco
Angeli.
Becattini G. (1995) *I sistemi industriali come strumento interpretativo dello
sviluppo italiano*, inaugural lecture, Fifth Meeting on Local
Development, Artimino
Bodo, G.and Viesti, G. (1997) *La grande svolta. Il Mezzogiorno nell'Italia
degli anni novanta.* Roma: Donzelli.
Braudel, F. (1984) "Presentazione," written for *Prato: storia di una città*,
typescript.
Capano, G. (1997) "L'ispessimento localizzato della filiera
agroalimentare come strumento di sviluppo" . In Flai-Cgil, ed.,
Sistemi locali di sviluppo agroindustriale nel Mezzogiorno, Roma: Lariser.
Centorrino, M.and Signorino, G. (1997) *Macroeconomia della mafia.*
Firenze: La Nuova Italia Scientifica.
Colorni, E. (1998) *Il coraggio dell'innocenza.* Napoli: La Città del Sole.
Colorni E. (2019) *Critical Thinking in Action.* New York: Bordighera
Press.
Colorni, E. (2021) *'The Philosophical Illness' and Other Writings.* New
York: Bordighera Press.

Corsi, C. (1994) *L'assistenza alla creazione d'impresa: l'esperienza del tutoraggio nella legge 44/86 attraverso casi empirici*, Naples, 1994

Coser, L.A. (1984) *Refugee Scholars in America. Their Impact and Their Experiences.* New Haven, Conn: Yale University Press.

Croce, B. (1973) *Scritti e discorsi politici 1943-1947.*Bari: Laterza.

De Filippo, E. (1975) "Vincenzo De Pretore," in *Le poesie di Eduardo.*Torino: Einaudi.

Frankfurt, H.G. (1971) "Freedom of the Will and the Concept of a Person". In *Journal of Philosophy*" n. 68,

Fumaroli, M. (1991) "L'Italie tridentine: une civilisation de otium", in *Commentaire*, n. 56.

Hirschman, A.O. (1948) "Economic and Financial Conditions in Italy". In *Review of Foreign Developments*, pp. 1-17.

Hirschman, A.O. (1958) *The Strategy of Economic Development.* New Haven, Conn.: Yale University Press.

Hirschman, A.O. (1967) *Development Projects Observed.* Washington DC: Brookings.

Hirschman, A.O. (1968) "Forward" to Tendler, J., *Electric Power in Brazil. Entrepreneurship in the Public Sector,* Cambridge MA: Harvard University Press.

Hirschman, A.O. (1970) *Exit, Voice, and Loyalty. Responses to Decline in Firms, Organizations, and States.* Cambridge Mass: Harvard Univ. Press.

Hirschman, A.O. (1971) *A Bias for Hope.* New Haven, Conn: Yale University Press.

Hirschman, A.O. (1973) "The Changing Tolerance for Income Inequality in the Course of Economic Development". *Quarterly Journal of Economics,* November.

Hirschman, A.O. (1974) "Exit, Voice, and Loyalty: Further Reflections and a Survey of Recent Contributions". In *Social Science Information.* 13 1: 121-141.

Hirschman, A.O. (1976) "Exit, Voice, and Loyalty. Comments". In *American Economic Review, Papers and Proceedings.*, 66: 386-389.

Hirschman, A.O. (1982) *Shifting Involvements: Private Interests and Public Action.*, Princeton NJ: Princeton Univ. Press.

Hirschman, A.O. (1984) *Getting Ahead Collectively. Experiences in Latin America.* New York: Pergamon.

Hirschman, A.O. (1985) "Against Parsimony: Three Easy Ways of Complicating Some Categories of Economic Discourse". In *Economics and Philosophy*, 1.

Hirschman, A. O. (1986) *Rival Views of Market Society and Other Recent Essays*. New York: Viking.

Harischman, A.O. (2022) *Three continents. Political Economy and Development of Democracy in Europe, the United States and Latin America*. New York: Peter Lang Publishers.

Hirschman, A.O. (1991) *The Rhetoric of Reaction*. Cambridge, Mass. Harvard University Press.

Hirschman, A.O. (1995) *A Propensity to Self-subversion*. Cambridge Mass: Harvard Univ. Press.

Hirschman A.O. (1998) *Crossing Boundaries.*New York:Zone Books.

Hirschman, A.O. (2020) *How Economics Should Be Complicated*. New York: Peter Lang Publisher.

La Palombara, J. (1987) *Democracy Italian Style*. New Haven, Conn: Yale University Press.

Maslow A. (1962) *Towards a Psychology of Being*, Princeton, N.J.: Van Nostrand

Meldolesi, L. (1990) "Mezzogiorno, con gioia". In *Nord e Sud*, n. 2.

Meldolesi, L. (1992) *Spender meglio è possibile*. Bologna: Il Mulino.

Meldolesi L. (1995) *Discovering the Possible. The Surprising World of Albert Hirschman.*Note Dame IN: Notre Dame University Press.

Meldolesi, L. (1996) "Mezzogiorno perduto e ritrovato". In *Sviluppo locale*, n. 2-3.

Meldolesi, L. (1998) *Dalla parte del Sud*. Bari-Roma: Laterza.

Meldolesi, L. (2000) *Occupazione ed emersione. Nuove proposte per il Mezzogiorno d'Italia*. Roma: Carocci.

Meldolesi, L. (2013) *Imparare ad imparare. Saggi d'incontro e di passione all'origine d'una possibile metamorfosi*. Soveria Mannelli: Rubbettino.

Meldolesi, L. (2019) "Ursula. Una nota". In Meldolesi, L., ed., *Taccuino italiano 1*. Roma: IDE.

Meldolesi, L. (2020) *Eppur si può*. Soveria Mannelli: Rubbettino.

Meldolesi, L. (2021) *Mezzogiorno con gioia!* Soveria Mannelli: Rubbettino

Meldolesi, L. (2022) *Protagonismi mediterranei*. Soveria Mannelli: Rubbettino.

Meldolesi, L, ed. (2019a) *Taccuino italiano 1*. Roma: IDE

Meldolesi, L., ed. (2019b) *Cambiamento che passione! Taccuino italiano n. 2*. Roma: IDE.

Meldolesi L. and Stame N., eds. (2019) *A Bias for Hope*. A Colorni-Hirschman International Institute Second Conference on Hirschman Legacy, The Word Bank.Roma: IDE.

Montesquieu (1965) *Les lettres persanes* .Paris: Flammarion.

Moro, G. (1998) *Crescita delle piccole imprese e sviluppo locale*. Mimeo.

Olson, M. (1965) *The Logic of Collective Action: Public Goods and the Theory of Group.*Cambridge, Mass: Harvard University Press.

Pezzino, P. (1992) *Il Paradiso abitato dai diavoli.*Milano: Franco Angeli.

Riotta, G. (1991) "Paisà d'America". In *7 – supplemento al Corriere della Sera*, 177.

Rokkan, S. (1974) "Introduction to 'Economics and Cultural Models of Comparative Policy-Making'. *Social Science Information*, n. 13.

Rokkan, S. (1975) "Dimension of State Formation and Nation Building: A Possible Paradigm for Research and Variations Within Europe" in Tilly, C., ed., *The Formation of National States in Western Europe*. Princeton NJ: Princeton University Press.

Rossi-Doria, M. (1982) *Scritti sul Mezzogiorno*. Torino: Einaudi.

Russo, G. (1997) *Il futuro è a Catania. Inchiesta su un'industria d'avanguardia in un'antica città del Sud*. Milano: Sperling.

Sen, A. (1977) "Rational Fools: a Critique of the Behavioural Foundations of Economic Theory". In *Philosophy and Public Affairs*, 6.

Serao, M. 1994) *Il ventre di Napoli*. Napoli: Casa Editrice Luca Torre.

Silone, I. (1968) *Emergency Exit* New York: Harper.

Trigilia, C. (1994) *Sviluppo senza autonomia. Effetti perversi delle politiche nel Mezzogiorno*. Bologna: Il Mulino.

Vidal, F. (1990) *Le management à l'italienne*. Paris: InterEditions.

ABOUT THE EDITOR

NICOLETTA STAME, sociologist: MA at SUNY — Binghamton; Assistant Professor at Paris X, Messina, Bari; Professor at Sapienza University of Roma until 2010.

Presently, vice-President of A Colorni-Hirschman International Institute. She is interested in democratic policies of development, particularly in the Mezzogiorno, also from the perspective of their evaluation that she approaches through a "possibilist" lens. She is past President of Associazione Italiana di Valutazione and of European Evaluation Society, and board member of *Evaluation*. Her published books in English are: *From Studies to Streams* (with R. Rist), *The Evaluation Enterprise* (with J.-E. Furubo), *Ethics for Evaluation: beyond "Doing no Harm" to "Tackling Bad and "Doing Good"* (with R.vdBerg and P. Hawkins), *Possibilism and Evaluation: Albert Hirschman and Judith Tendler*.

IL NOSTRO MEZZOGIORNO

This series is dedicated to new perspectives on how we might reconsider Southern Italy and the Mediterranean.

Luca Meldolesi. *An America in Antiquity? Mediterranean Perspectives: "La pensée de midi" and "Our Mezzogiorno".* ISBN 978-1-59954-207-2.

EDITORIAL GROUP

www.ingramcontent.com/pod-product-compliance
Lightning Source LLC
Chambersburg PA
CBHW031432270326
41930CB00007B/671